THE MYSTERY THAT IS

MARS

By

Rob Shelsky

Other books by Rob Shelsky include:

Darker Side Of The Moon "They" Are Watching Us! A nonfiction book on the dangers UFOs present.

Time Travel Invasion, a nonfiction book on the real possibility that time travel may already exist.
For The Moon Is Hollow And Aliens Rule The Sky, a nonfiction book on the hollow moon theory.

Ancient Alien Empire, Megalithia, a nonfiction book that documents evidence of an ancient alien civilization on Earth.

Deadly UFOs And The Disappeared, a nonfiction book about the danger presented by UFOs.

Mysteries Of Time Travel: 35 Cases Of Time Travel Intrusion, a nonfiction book about time travel.'

Mysteries Of Mothman, a nonfiction book about the phenomenon known as the Mothman.

And many more!

* * * * *

~ DEDICATION ~

For

George Kempland 1929—2013

Friend, mentor, and so much more.
May we someday, somewhen meet again.
I wish to acknowledge you for all your kindness,
generosity, and help.

Thank you so very much!

Contents

INTRODUCTION

"No one would have believed in the last years of the nineteenth century that this world was being watched keenly and closely by intelligences greater than man's..."

—H.G. Wells, *War of the Worlds*

MARS—our mysterious neighbor! For centuries, it has been an enigma. Moreover, when humans don't know something, their imaginations can run wild. This is just what has happened with Mars over the past several centuries and it has happened to an incredible extent.

Some of those imaginings have been seemingly very farfetched, indeed, as with H.G. Wells' novel, *War of the Worlds*. Another famous author, Edgar Rice Burroughs also created a strange world, one that had deserts and canals, strange creatures, and marvelous inventions unknown on our planet.

There have been many other such scenarios in fiction relating to Mars and by many other authors over the decades that followed these two men. Movies, too, have done this, and often they are horror films. Either Martians seem to be invading Earth in such movies, or monsters kill hapless astronauts when they land on Mars. In short, Mars has been given the short end of the stick when it comes to just what kind of life might have developed there, and how we humans could interact with it. Far more often than not, Martians, for us humans at least, are monsters.

However, over the last 100 years, this has finally begun to change and our understanding of just what kind of planet Mars is, has become more rational in nature, or so many of us thought. As our technology has grown, so has our knowledge of the red planet. Yet oddly, even as we find more answers, we find that we have even created more questions about Mars than we had before! In addition, some of those questions are monumental ones, and perhaps just as strange as Mr. Burroughs' version of the planet, or H.G. Wells' idea of it from his book, *War of the Worlds.*

Additionally, this time, our imaginings are not just restricted to the world of fiction. Scientists, too, have often come up with different ideas about Mars and some of these are "really out there." Other scientists, of course, have refuted these so-called flights of fantasy, and have often tried to keep Mars as just another planet, one that is mundane in its makeup, and not so very different from Earth in many ways.

That is, in many ways, but not all, it seems. Mars differs from Earth in some very fundamental and peculiar ways, ones that we couldn't predict 100 years ago. In fact, it turns out that Mars, the reality that is the planet, is indeed much stranger than fiction.

Moreover, it seems to be getting stranger by the year. We are finding some bizarre things, things for which scientists simply can't account, not only on the surface of Mars, but even on one of its moons. Then there is the matter of the Russian photographs of what appears to be a huge cylindrical ship plying the space between Phobos and Mars itself. Other photographs of the surface of the Red Planet also show bizarre, out-of-place objects. We will discuss that more later on.

We can go further. What was once thought a dead world may have life after all, including not only on the microbial level, but also on the large level, as well, if some of the photographic evidence we've seen is correct. In short, life may be there on Mars and in abundance. What's more, there might even be intelligent life...of some sort.

As bizarre as all this may sound, we have even more questions to answer about the planet. For instance, and these are just some:

Are Ancient Alien theorists right about Mars? Did They Once Visit Earth?

Did another civilization once occupy our neighboring world?

Was Earth, as some scientists theorize, populated by life from Mars?

Is there ancient evidence of a terrible war or catastrophe on the planet?

Are aliens still occupying the red planet?

Did Mars once have a different orbit?

Is the moon, Phobos, in reality some sort of spaceship?

Is there one or more advanced alien species still alive on Mars?

Do we need to fear our neighboring planet and what secrets it may yet hold?

Are there secret human bases on Mars

Is there a secret space fleet?

Whether any of these turn out to be true or not, these are just some of the questions we need answers to and soon! Time is running out. With regular trips to Mars, manned Mars explorations in the planning, we need to know just what we might be facing. At the very least, we have to understand what we might inadvertently bring back to Earth that might be deadly to us!

In this book, *The Mystery That Is Mars,* we will consider the available evidence. Each facet of Mars will be explored in an orderly and systematic manner. We will cover each of the questions above and more besides. Thus, we will sort through all the data and attempt to arrive at some conclusions with regard to all these questions. Ultimately, you, the reader, must decide for yourself if the evidence warrants such conclusions.

Why do we need to know if our sister planet, Mars, is just another world somewhat like our own, and one which harbors little that is dangerous, or if indeed, the planet was named aptly for the God Mars, the God of War. Why is it important to do this?

The answer is simple: because our lives and even our future as a species may depend upon finding those very answers. In this book, I will provide information about Mars, what scientist know, as well as what they *think* they may know.

However, I will go further. I am also including a great deal of material about some of the anomalous things about Mars, and some of it is truly bizarre and frightening in ways. Furthermore, I will also cover some of the major conspiracy theories about the red planet, as well. I will attempt to draw conclusions based on available evidence that seems to be solid. These conclusions might not be yours and I do not intend to try to force my opinions about them on anyone.

Instead, what I would like the reader to do is to read the book. Consider the facts contained therein. Consider the evidence. Reflect on the theories provided, their merits, and weaknesses. Reflect on my conclusions about them. Then, arrive at your own conclusions about it all.

One thing I will say; given the available evidence about Mars now, you might just find my conclusions, and your own, as well, not only "out there," but also alarming, perhaps even terrifying...so, let's get started!

PART I—THE FACTS

CHAPTER 1—The Origin Of Mars

The first thing we need to discuss is how Mars came to be Mars and why it is where it is. Scientists used to believe that our solar system was very much like the inner workings of a clock, which ran smoothly since the solar system's formation. They refer to the fact of the early system having an accretion disk of dust, debris, and gases. All this swirled around our young sun in a huge flat disk.

Gradually, over time, this disk, thanks to radiation from our young sun acting as a form of pressure in the form of a solar wind caused such particles to push outward against the debris, gasses, etc. This caused the material to become denser. As density increased, gravity came into strong effect. Clumps of debris collided and sometimes grew in size. Their increased gravity attracted even more debris and there was no shortage of this at the time. Finally, this debris, gas, and dust accreted into planets, or at least protoplanets. These "protoplanets," these gathering balls of dust and rubble, slowly grew in size. Some struck others and were destroyed. Others coalesced and grew even larger.

As they grew, their gravitational attraction continued to grow along with them. They attracted even more material yet. Eventually, the various planets formed. After their formation, they went on swinging around the sun for the next 4-1/2 billion years or so, in their present orbits until today. If the early solar system was chaotic, cosmologists and astronomers felt it quickly became an ordered existence, a nicely running sort of clockwork solar mechanism.

This was the original theory based on the facts as known at the time scientists formulated it. This is what teachers taught me as a child in my science classes.

The universe, and particularly our solar system, was just like some giant and intricate clockwork mechanism. In fact, there once was a theory of the universe called just that, the Clockwork Theory, although this applied to the whole universe and not just our solar system. Even so, the theory applied to our system, as well.

However, times do change. We've uncovered new facts and evidence. Although, still not considered wrong, the accretion theory has had some major modifications and adjustments made to it. For example, it seems the early solar system was far more chaotic than even we once thought.

Yes, protoplanets apparently did roll along in orbits around the sun, but constant collisions with others, or the close gravitational attraction of them, often sent the early protoplanets careening off onto new paths, some to dive into the sun, some to exit the solar system forever as rogue planets, and some to crash into each other. It is theorized this happened with Earth, and that a protoplanet the approximate size of Mars (called "Theia") impacted our Earth, thus creating the Moon. However, even with this theory there are problems, so we still just consider it a theory and not an absolute fact. As a theory, it might just have to undergo even more modifications yet, consequently.

In other words, the early solar system was an incredibly chaotic place, with perhaps hundreds or even thousands of proto-planets forming, colliding with each other, being destroyed—some forever—some reforming once more. In short, the early solar system was rather like some crazy and complex game of celestial pinball. Earth was involved in this disordered muddle and suffered the consequences, as did Mars, according to current theories.

Mars, it is believed, suffered from her big brother, Jupiter, being so close to her. Jupiter, that largest gas giant of a planet in our solar system was like a huge vacuum cleaner, or so scientists tell us. It grew quickly and sucked up debris around it in a huge swath. Jupiter's gravitational pull kept growing even as the planet's mass did, allowing it to gather up even more rubble.

In any event, many scientists say this left less for Mars to accumulate in the way of material, but accumulate what it could, it did. Some researchers say it only took around 100,000 years for this accretion of Mars to occur. Even so, stunted because of being so close to her greedy nearest neighbor, Jupiter, Mars ended up being a smaller world. In fact, it is much smaller than its terrestrial (rocky-like) sisters, Earth and Venus.

Despite this fact, many researchers now believe early Mars was much warmer and wetter than it is today, judging by the available evidence Mars missions have retrieved. Supposedly, it had a much thicker atmosphere with great amounts of carbon dioxide in it. This would cause warming of the planet, since carbon dioxide is a greenhouse gas that traps sunlight and just in the same way as a glass greenhouse might. Therefore, Mars was warm, wrapped in a thick atmosphere as it was. This allowed the surface to hold liquid water. As we will see later in this book, the planet probably even had some shallow oceans, as well as rivers and lakes early on in the planet's history.

Then, as Mars lost its atmosphere, being small, with its gravity too weak to hold it, and a disappearing magnetosphere allowing the solar wind to blow the atmosphere away, the planet grew colder and drier over time. The atmosphere thinned.

This, on the face of it, is a good theory, but like most theories of our solar system, it is not without some problems, some of them major ones. Here are some of the main ones:

1. Mars does not seem to possess much in the way of high concentrations of carbonates. Carbonates should be there in abundance if the early atmosphere was so very full of carbon dioxide. This gas should have combined in chemical reactions over time, at least in part, to form other compounds, such as those carbonates. These should have been deposited on the surface of the planet. Again, that does not seem to have been the case to any real extent. We simply don't find much in the way of carbonates there, certainly, not as much as there should be if this theory is correct.

As proof of this, on Earth, we have many carbonates because of our carbon dioxide. So where did all the carbon dioxide go on Mars, if not into carbonates? Long before most of the once thick atmosphere was lost, the chemical processes should have left plenty of carbonates behind for us now to discover.

Therefore, some scientists think Mars might have once had an orbit closer in to the sun where it was warmer and then it migrated farther out, even as Jupiter is said to have done (first migrating in toward the sun, and then Jupiter migrating out again due to the influence of Saturn). We have no idea if any of these theories are valid at this point. They are really just our best guesses.

2. The orbit of Mars is highly elliptical, whereas Earth has a nearly perfect circular orbit, and one that is barely elliptical in nature. Venus, too, has very close to a circular orbit. Something has influenced in a rather dramatic fashion the orbit of Mars, apparently, so that it is no longer like this.

3. Neither does Mars orbit the sun in quite the same plane as Earth or Venus, or the other planets. When the early accretion disk of dust, gasses, and debris orbited our sun, it was in a flattish plane, with all the planets forming in that same disk/plane. However, Mars is a bit off from that. Some scientists feel it is the closeness of the giant planet, Jupiter, that has caused this effect, and yet, that is only a hypothesis.

4. The planet Mars is quite small (please see comparison image later in this book) and some scientists say that at its present size, it really shouldn't have any atmosphere to speak of at all...or ever! Although it is a thin atmosphere now, they argue it should be a good deal thinner yet, or virtually nonexistent. Our moon, which is quite large (although not as large as Mars, certainly), has no atmosphere at all, for example.

The problem with this idea is that one of the theories behind Mars losing its atmosphere is the result of an impact by a large object, such as a huge asteroid. Such researchers point to the surface features of Mars, which they say shows such an impact did take place. The blast would have made Mars lose much of its atmosphere. Assuming, of course, little Mars had a thicker one in the first place, but many scientists believe it did.

The majority of scientists also argue it was the loss of its protective magnetic field and the resulting power of the solar wind that drove the atmosphere away from the world. That and with the weakness of the small planet's gravitational pull, Mars was unable to hold onto its air over the long term.

Either way, both theories call for the Martian atmosphere as having once been much heavier and so warmer. The fact the planet could well have had oceans at one time, would require such a thicker atmosphere, or the seas would either never have formed, or quickly evaporated. Yet, again, such a small world, one so near the asteroid belt and the resulting impacts from many random asteroids nearby, shouldn't really have had such a thick atmosphere for very long. Yet, we think it once did have this and for quite some time.

How do we resolve the issue? To date, we have more questions than answers about this problem. Our evidence shows one thing; a thick atmosphere and probably oceans, but we have no answers as to how this could have been or have existed there for so long a time.

What we do know is Mars seems in many respects to be a sister planet to Earth, having formed in much the same way (maybe), and yet, it is markedly and rather strangely different in other ways, as well, including its atmosphere, apparently.

Finally, there are other theories of the formation of Mars, including one that involves a destroyed planet, Phaeton, or Phaëton, and sometimes even called Phaethon. This was a planet theorized to have once been between Mars and Jupiter, where the asteroid belt exists now (the remnants of Phaeton, as it is theorized by some). Some researchers think that either Mars was once a part of this Phaeton and was shot off from it after Phaeton was destroyed in some catastrophe (various causes for this catastrophe have been theorized), or the death throes of Phaeton caused a heavy bombardment, or even collisions with Mars, thus damaging its atmosphere, as well as the planet, itself.

This would account for the relatively small size of Mars, being just a "chunk" of its mother world as it were, its eccentric orbit, and its orbit, and even not being quite in the same plane as that of Earth's orbit. The residue of Phaeton that became Mars had been blown into this elliptical orbit and plane. It might also account for Mars once having had a much thicker atmosphere and water, since it was once part of a larger planet having all this and so only lost it after that planet, Phaeton, was destroyed. We simply do not know one way or the other, but we will discuss this more in depth in a later chapter.

Chapter Conclusion: Whether or not any of this last is true, or even partially true is a matter of conjecture. However, some scientists feel that Phaeton might have actually existed. Where its orbit was more or less predicted to be, a number of very large asteroids have been discovered, including Ceres, Juno, Pallas, and Vesta, all much bigger than average asteroids. With the migration of the planets Jupiter and later Saturn in their orbits, they theorize that gravitational/tidal forces from these giants or from some "internal" force or forces within the planet might have torn Phaeton apart. This left a debris field, the Asteroid Belt, where the planet once orbited, and with the largest pieces now forming the bigger asteroids in that same orbit.

The truth is we simply don't know how Mars ultimately came to be, or what exactly stripped it of its atmosphere, why it is much smaller than Earth or Venus, or why it has an eccentric orbit, and in a slightly different plane from Earth. Yet all these things are true, and somehow, someway, we have to account for them.

What makes this accounting difficult is new information keeps coming in, and it is always adding to our knowledge, but also adding to our questions about Mars. The more odd data we get, the more we stretch to try to explain it all. There is no doubt most scientist think Mars simply formed from an accretion disk and then was negatively influenced by the closeness of giant Jupiter. This is possibly true, but again, even this theory doesn't explain all the facts, like the lack of carbonates being in abundance on Mars. These are all oddities for which we cannot yet account.

Several researchers have hypothesized different explanations for the current state of our solar system, including Immanuel Velikovsky in his book on the subject, *Worlds In Collision*, which most scientists refute as just a form of pseudo-science. Whether or not Velikovsky might actually be right, or at least partially right, is still a subject for some very real debate. Even so, his work does explain some of the oddities we see in our solar system.

In the next chapter, we will focus on these oddities, especially those of Mars in more detail, and after that, the odd moon of Mars, Phobos, as well. As we shall see, the oddities just don't stop coming...

CHAPTER 2—Some Basic Facts About Mars

Before we get started, it is necessary to consider the red planet itself. We need to understand what we already know about it. This information will act as a starting point for us. We have to be able to discern what we're talking about here and what might be different or strange about our sister world as compared to our own. So, let's get started.

Here are some basic facts we now know about Mars:

1. Mars, like Earth, Venus, and Mercury is a terrestrial world. This means it is rocky-like, rather than like Jupiter or Saturn, which are gas giants. Like Earth, Mars has an atmosphere, but it is much thinner than Earth's. The Martian atmosphere is mostly composed of carbon dioxide, although there are other trace gases as well. In fact, we would not be able to breathe the air of Mars, because it is about 96% carbon dioxide and only contains about 0.2% oxygen as opposed to 21% oxygen here on Earth. We would gasp like fish out of water on Mars.

2. Mars is the farthest rocky world from the sun, being the fourth out. Moreover, as rocky worlds go, there is only one smaller than it, and that is Mercury, closest planet to the sun.

3. Many people often typically refer to Mars as the red planet, because as seen from Earth, it has a distinctly reddish color. This is because much of the surface of Mars is reddish. This tint is due to oxidized iron compounds, or in other words, types of rust. The Romans associated this color with blood. The ancient Chinese referred to Mars as "the fire star," for the same reason, it's uniquely red coloration. Even to our naked eyes, the planet, seen as a star in our skies, looks reddish.

4. The planet has two moons, Phobos, and Deimos. Both are quite small compared to our moon.

5. Where the Earth is one astronomical unit from the sun, or approximately 93 million miles, or 149.6 million kilometers, Mars is about 1.52 astronomical units from the sun. That is, it is 141.6 million miles, or 228 million kilometers. At its closest point to us, Mars is 33.9 million miles, or 54.6 million kilometers away from us. This is an approximation because the distance varies depending upon where Earth and Mars are in relation to each other in their orbits around the sun at any given time.

6. Mars takes almost 2 years to orbit the sun, just about twice as long as the Earth does. That is, about 1.9 Earth years, or 687 of our Earth days.

7. The first recorded historical mention of Mars was by Egyptian astronomers in approximately the Second Millennium BC.

8. By our standards, Mars is generally a very cold world. Its surface temperature can be as low as a minus 153 or so degrees centigrade (or -243°F), but it can, on occasion in summertime (summer on Mars, that is), get as high as 20°C (68°F). Therefore, at those times, in the peak of summer at the equator on Mars, one could be comfortable in shirtsleeves. That is, except for the lack of oxygen, deadly carbon dioxide atmosphere and the harsh solar radiation and cosmic rays that strike the surface of that world, which would be fatal to the unprotected in very short order.

Now we come to some peculiar and rather interesting facts about Mars:

9. Earth and Mars share about the same area of usable land. Despite Mars being a small world, being only about 15% of the earth and its volume is just a mere 10% of Earth's mass; Mars has no oceans or seas now. Therefore, all of its land is, theoretically, available for use. However, because of the small size of Mars, its gravity is considerably less than Earth, being just a little over one-third of our world. Therefore, like the Moon, if you chose to jump, you could jump much higher than on Earth. On Mars, that would be about three times higher than you could here.

A comparison of Mars in size to Earth.
Source: NASA

10. Another interesting fact is Mars is home to the largest volcano in the solar system, of any planet or moon in it, for that matter. This monster is Olympus Mons. Olympus Mons is a shield volcano and it rises approximately 21 kilometers above the surface of the planet. Moreover, it is some 600 kilometers in diameter. The thing is huge by any standards for volcanoes!

Current evidence indicates the volcano actually might still be active, because some lava flows from it seemed to have occurred recently in history. So high is Olympus Mons, that some scientists say it actually rises above the thin layer of atmosphere on Mars. In other words, the peak of that volcano actually sticks out into the vacuum of space. This is strange, that such a small world would have the solar system's biggest volcano....

11. Mars is a difficult world to get to, in fact more difficult than our other neighboring planet, Venus. Missions to Mars had been mostly unsuccessful if you look at the numbers. Out of 40 missions to the planet, only 18 have managed to arrive or land there successfully. I only include missions that went directly to Mars here, and not ones that just passed by it on their way to somewhere else. Altogether, though, there were some 68 missions. The first such mission started its journey to the red planet in 1960. Moreover, it isn't just the United States having had this problem of so many failed missions. All the other countries that have tried have had such problems, as well.

12. Mars may not have much of an atmosphere, but it is home to the largest dust storms of any world in our solar system. Sometimes they are planet wide and can go on for long periods.

13. As mentioned, Mars has rather an odd orbit. It is highly oval-shaped, or elliptical. This is even more so than just about any other planet in our solar system, but it is not quite the most extreme in this respect. Still, there are questions as to why the orbit of our sister planet is so eccentric.

14. Mars has two moons. One of them, the moon, Phobos, is destined to die. In a mere 22 to perhaps 40 million years (figures vary on this), a mere blink of the eye in geological times, the strange moon, Phobos, will get too close to Mars and be torn asunder. It will probably end as a thin ring of debris around that planet before disappearing entirely. The bombardment of Mars by pieces of Phobos would not make a pleasant spot for vacation during that time.

15. Mars has a very similar sort of tilt to it compared to Earth, that is, a 25° tilt on its axis, while our planet has a 23.5° tilt. This means that Mars has seasons just as we do here on Earth, although they are each almost twice as long as ours are. The odd thing about this tilt is that we believe our Moon helps keep Earth at a reasonable angle, acting as a stabilizer for Earth in this respect.

Without this stabilizing effect, scientists theorize the Earth could just go on tilting, even ending up on its side and so sort of "rolling" along in its orbit around the sun. In other words, our planet would tilt at all angles over time, and disastrously so for life on our planet. Yet, despite having no moon of any size capable of acting as such a stabilizer, Mars still has very much the same tilt as our world and seems to have had this for some long time...why this is so, we do not know.

16. Ancient Mars had water, apparently lots of it. Many scientists agree on this fact. The question seems to be for how long it had this water. Moreover, just how much of it was there? Again, many scientists think Mars actually had an ocean at one time and a much thicker atmosphere to go with it. This means Mars was once warmer and wet!

17. The evidence now indicates from satellites orbiting Mars that there is still water! Photographs show what appear to be seasonal flows. Whether this is a highly salty water, or fresh is a matter of conjecture. There is also water in the form of ice at the Polar Regions in the frozen soil there. Furthermore, there is even evidence that where a probe landed, there is water in the soil. A photograph shows what appears to be a water spot evaporating from underneath the craft at the landing site, if only a trace amount. Even so, there must be water there, if only in small amounts!

Ancient Mars with seas?
Image Source: NASA

18. Mars has a huge canyon that dwarfs the American Grand Canyon in size and depth, because not only is it the most massive such canyon known on any planet in our Solar System, but it is the deepest, as well. The Valles Marineris, as named, is almost as wide as the United States, being some 3,000 kilometers in length, and up to eight kilometers in depth in various places.

Compare this to our Grand Canyon, which is only 800 kilometers in length and less than two kilometers deep at its lowest points. The Valles Marineris, its cause, is a mystery. How the thing formed is still unknown. Some scientists once theorized that it formed as Mars cooled and shrunk in size, thus leaving a large crease or crack in its surface crust, but this has since been pretty much discounted. There does seem to be some ongoing geological activity in the canyon. There are other theories as to its formation and we shall discuss those later on this book.

View of Valles Marineris, "the Grand Canyon
 of Mars
Source: NASA

Another View of Valles Marineris
Source: Wikimedia

Chapter Conclusion: Although scientists once considered Mars a sort of "failed Earth," we now know that our sister world is much more varied in its makeup than we thought. We also have seen some surprising differences between Mars and Earth, and yet some marked similarities, as well, such as its axial tilt, for example. Mars is a world of mystery in its own right. In addition, there are some very strange peculiarities about the planet. We will discuss these in more depth later on in this book.

In any case, now that we've seen the basics about Mars, let's look at its moons, especially the weird little moon, Phobos.

CHAPTER 3—The Weird Moon, Phobos

Now we come to the moons of Mars, Phobos, and Deimos. These are Greek names, with Phobos meaning fear, and Deimos meaning panic or terror (depending on one's translation). The names came from the horses of the god, Mars, (or the Greek version, "Ares") and they, according to legend, hauled the chariot of that god. Since Mars was the god of war, the names fear and terror are fitting appellations for those moons.

Deimos does not seem to be anything too out of the ordinary as far as we can currently tell, although, its origin just might be. For a long time, scientists thought that both moons of Mars were actually captured asteroids, but this is now a major question and/or a point of dispute. The orbits of both moons do not seem to fit with their having been captured and pulled into orbit around Mars from the Asteroid Belt. Captured objects tend to have erratic or eccentric orbits. The orbits of both Deimos and Phobos are quite circular.

Therefore, scientists are now unsure just what their origins might be, or where they initially came from. However, the moon, Phobos, definitely has a spectroscopic analysis that is consistent with the idea it might have been an asteroid, since the analysis is similar to those of asteroids, but it has certain problems in this regard, as well, which we will touch on later.

Deimos is small, even smaller than Phobos, being only around 9.9 miles, or 11 kilometers long. These figures vary some, depending on the source, but are not far apart. It takes about 30 hours to orbit Mars. When viewed, the moon seems little more than a cratered rock. However, being some 14,573 miles, or 23,460 kilometers from Mars, the moon, Deimos, is over twice again as far from the planet as Phobos is.

Phobos is by far and away the more bizarre moon of the two. It has some very singular oddities about it. First, though, let's start with a few basic facts about that moon:

1. Like its sister moon, Deimos, Phobos was discovered by Asaph Hall, an astronomer of the late 1800s. He found the moons in 1877.

2. Again, Phobos is aptly named as a companion to Mars, the God of War, since it is the Greek word for "fear" (as in "phobia). The moon is not large, although it is approximately seven times larger than Deimos. Again, Phobos orbits Mars much closer in than Deimos. Phobos does not have a spherical shape, rather being lumpy and irregular in its contours. This is one of the reasons why some think it to be a captured asteroid, since as mentioned, it closely resembles asteroids in the Asteroid Belt in this regard. The moon has a spectroscopic analysis similar to that of a carbonaceous chondrite asteroid (C-type asteroid), which further lends support to the idea it might have been an asteroid. Yet, there are oddities here, too…

3. Phobos has some weird characteristics. The moon orbits a mere 6,000 kilometers, or about 3,700 mi from the surface of the planet. So close is this, that the moon orbits the red planet four times a day! This makes it the closest moon to a planet in our Solar System by far. In fact, Phobos makes a full orbit of the planet in just seven hours and thirty-nine minutes. So quickly does Phobos zip around Mars that it goes much faster than the red planet can rotate. This means that from the ground, Phobos rises in the west and crosses the sky in just about four hours and 15 minutes. This also means it sets in the east!

4. Another oddity about Phobos is that it has a very low albedo, meaning it doesn't reflect light well very well at all. In fact, Phobos is one of the worst reflecting moons or worlds in our solar system. The moon's albedo is just 0.071, which is extremely low. Considered airless, the surface temperature of Phobos ranges from a high of minus four degrees centigrade, when receiving direct sunlight, to a -112 degrees centigrade in areas not receiving such light.

5. Phobos has a singularly large crater, Stickney Crater, and this feature dominates the moon's landscape. The crater is big, being about 9 kilometers or a little over five-and-one-half miles in its diameter. So big is the impact crater, scientists think it must have come close to destroying the little moon when the meteorite hit. Inside the crater is an even smaller impact crater. This tells us that Stickney is older, having had to form first.

6. There is also a feature known as "the monolith," a strange outcrop, or jutting monument of rock on the moon. This is roughly rectangular in shape.

7. There are also "grooves" on part of the moon's surface. These grooves virtually cover Phobos. Most seem to be about 30 meters or about 98 feet deep and appear to be anywhere from 100 to around 200 meters wide. They do seem remarkably consistent in this respect. The grooves are up to 20 kilometers in length (about 12 miles, approximately). At first thought to be rays (streaks of debris thrown out by the impact that created Stickney Crater), this has since been reconsidered, and because they do not radiate out from the crater as such rays should. Nor do they look like "rays" in any case. Rays are usually the result of debris cast from a crater, but these are actual grooves in the surface of the little moon.

Images taken by the Mars Express Explorer craft show the grooves seem to have the main summit of Phobos as their center, and not the crater. This, too, would detract from the idea they are rays from Stickney Crater.

Researchers can't account for this either, other than to surmise that the grooves are the results of debris thrown from successive meteor impacts with the moon, thus forming a "chain" of craters that appear now as grooves. Nobody really can account for why these craters should be in such chain formations. Moreover, when looking at the grooves, nobody knows why they should be in such neat parallel lines, so they are still a major question that way, as well. (See images below.) Some of the grooves do seem to be those chains of craters, judging by images taken by various spacecraft, but others do not. Others seem to be just regular grooves. Again, whether just grooves, or crater chains, nobody knows how they could have come about.

8. Phobos has a very low density for its size. In fact, it is too low according to most scientists. Scientists estimate the mass of Phobos to be 1.0659×10^{16} kg (1.78477 nEarths), and its mean density to be just 1.876 g/cm^3, which is quite low, too low for Phobos to be solid by all accounts.

This has raised the question as to whether Phobos might be hollow, or have a high porosity. Some astronomers conjecture it might actually be more a pile of loose rubble barely held together with only a shallow crust as an overlay, acting as a binding force for it all. However, since it has definite and seemingly permanent features on the surface, this remains a big question, because such a loose collection of "rubble" should shift and change with time. Moreover, how could it survive an impact such as that created by whatever formed the Stickney Crater if it was just a loose collection of rubble barely held together?

Therefore, others feel it may truly be hollow. Some even claim it could well be an alien spaceship disguised as an asteroid, or even hollowed out from one and then placed into such a neat and circular orbit around Mars for some sort of observational purposes.

Still others think there may be a good amount of water trapped in the little moon, and this could account for its low density. However, data on the surface material, known as regolith, shows no hydration (water content) of any significance at all, so this, too, is still just a theory and one with little evidence to support it. Those same scientists now theorize that perhaps the water is residing below the dry outer crust. This water would most likely be in the form of ice, if so.

9. As mentioned, Phobos may be "temporary." Unlike Deimos, Phobos is tightening its orbit around Mars, moving closer to it by about one meter every hundred years. Although this may not seem like a lot, it has consequences. This means that ultimately, if this continues, Phobos will either crash into Mars, or tear itself apart (most likely event) as it gets too close to Mars and so then form a thin ring of debris around the planet for a time, before disappearing completely as the fragments rain down upon the planet over the millennia. Estimates vary on the moon's ultimate disastrous fate with some saying as little as 11 million years, and some saying it will be closer to 44 to 50 million years, depending on circumstances.

Phobos
Source: NASA

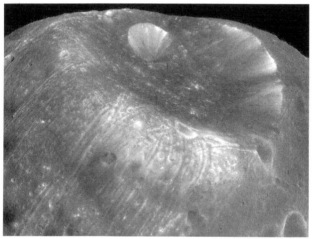

Impact Crater, Stickney
Source: NASA

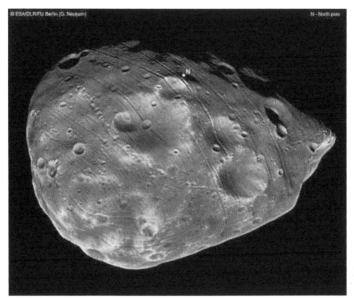

Odd shaped Phobos with grooves prominently shown
Source: NASA

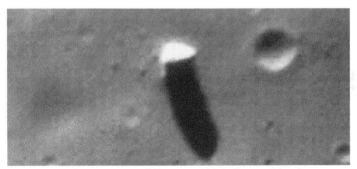

Image close-up of "monolith" on Phobos
Source: NASA

10. There is an absence of dust rings. Astronomers think Phobos should have a 100-meter layer of dust or regolith on its surface, although there is little actual evidence to support this theory. If there is such a layer, it means (or has been predicted by scientists several times) that both Phobos, and its sister moon, Deimos, should have some sort of dust rings around them. Yet, none has been discovered at all to date, despite many attempts in this regard to find them.

In addition, it is unknown how such a thick layer of dust/regolith could be on the surface of Phobos. The belief is the dust is the result of numerous meteor impacts over the ages, but there is a problem; Phobos is so small, its gravity is so minimal that scientists can't account for how the dust and debris would stay on the moon's surface.

When the meteor/asteroid impacts occurred, it should have just exploded back out into space because of so little gravity acting to hold it there. For instance, a human weight of about 150 pounds would only weigh about two ounces on Phobos. The weight of some small particles of dust would be negligible by comparison, virtually zero, and certainly not enough to be captured by the little moon. This means the rebound after impact should have allowed the dust to reach escape velocity from Phobos (the speed required to escape the tiny amount of gravity Phobos does possess).

Chapter Conclusion: Like Mars, there is much about Phobos that is truly weird and there is much that scientists don't know or cannot account for at this point. However, there are theories which just might provide answers and we will discuss those later on in this book.

PART II—A QUESTION OF LIFE ON MARS?

CHAPTER 4—Was There Once Life On Mars?

Now that we've covered the basic facts of Mars and its moons, we need to move further afield. We need to consider some less certain matters about Mars before we then go on to discuss some truly weird things about the planet itself, its moon, Phobos, and some major theories regarding just what might be going on around the planet.

First, let's consider the following:

Was there once life on Mars, and/or is there now? Let's go with the first part of this question first, with regard to ancient Mars having had life. Did it? Well, nobody knows for certain, but there is a very good chance it did. Researchers base this on the following suppositions:

1. Life seems to thrive everywhere on Earth where it seems remotely possible for it to do so. From searing, boiling temperatures near fumaroles (volcanic-like vents) in the depths of our deepest oceans to high in the atmosphere, life exists on Earth in many forms. Moreover, life, at least certain forms of it (microbial, virus, spores, etc.) seem to be able even to survive in the harsh conditions of the vacuum of space for long periods.

This is no small feat! Space, as most people know, is a vacuum. It is subject to incredibly cold temperatures, and harsh radiation, as well as extreme heat when something is in sunlight. Space is not a pleasant place for life, obviously. Yet, experiments aboard the International Space Station have shown some forms of life, if only on the microbial and/or viral and spore level, do seem to be able to survive for long periods in such horribly harsh conditions.

2. As mentioned earlier, Mars, according to many scientists was a warmer and wetter place. In fact, it was amazingly Earth-like at one time they say, complete with land, sea, lakes, and rivers. This means there should have been enough water there for life to develop. In addition, life does seem to need water; at least, it does here on Earth and that's all we have to go by.

3. Mars also had a much thicker atmosphere, it seems. This means life had protection, was protected from harsh solar radiation and cosmic rays. This, too, would help life develop.

4. Mars apparently once had a planetary magnetic field, or magnetosphere, as it is called. This, too, would have helped protect life as it developed on the planet, since the magnetic field surrounding Mars would have shield such life from harmful cosmic rays and effects of the solar wind.

In short, if life develops the same way everywhere in the universe as it does on Earth, requires the same sorts of environments and necessities, there is no reason, given that Mars once had all the necessities for life in abundance that life shouldn't have evolved there. This would be just as it did on Earth. Moreover, some scientists, mainstream ones, theorize that life on Earth might have originated from life on Mars.

The upshot of all this is, Mars should have at least begun to develop life a long time ago, longer ago than it did on Earth, because Mars cooled faster than our primeval planet did (being smaller and farther from the sun than Earth).

Do we have any solid evidence for this having happened? As it happens, we do. This knowledge hasn't come easily to us. Yet, the more we learn about the red planet, the more we begin to believe life had to at least, once have existed on Mars. We think this because of several factors:

1. Martian Meteorites. Some Martian meteorites, blown off that planet by asteroid and/or large meteor impacts, have made their way to Earth over millions of years. These are old meteorites, ones having spent a long time in space, perhaps billions of years even, as some scientists think. Yet, in a NASA report released in August of 1996, at the Johnson Space Center in Texas, and at Stanford University, researchers showed evidence of what appeared to be fossilized remains (microscopic) in one such ancient meteorite.

Now at first, this was highly disputed by many scientists at the time, was the subject of much controversy, but over the years after having had the pendulum of disputes swing in both directions, many scientists now think the find was real. Many now feel the microscopic fossils of bacteria-like creatures are just that, fossils.

Moreover, their origin is Mars! If not exactly "cast-in-concrete" evidence, even so, this lends strong credence, is definitely compelling data supporting the idea that, at least, primitive life once inhabited Mars sometime in the ancient past. Scientists theorize this must have been around three-and-a-half billion years ago. This find was reported in the *Science Journal*.

Additionally, the evidence from this meteorite was not just from one single bit of data, but rather many. As one researcher put it:

"There is not any one finding that leads us to believe that this is evidence of past life on Mars. Rather, it is a combination of many things that we have found."

This was the Johnson Space Center planetary scientist. Dr. David McKay who said this also said:

"They include Stanford's detection of an apparently unique pattern of organic molecules, carbon

compounds that are the basis of life. We also found several unusual mineral phases that are known products of primitive microscopic organisms on Earth. Structures that could be microscopic fossils seem to support all of this. The relationship of all of these things in terms of location—within a few hundred thousandths of an inch of one another—is the most compelling evidence."

In addition, Professor of Chemistry, Dr. Richard Zare at Stanford University said:

"It is very difficult to prove life existed 3.6 billion years ago on Earth, let alone on Mars. The existing standard of proof, which we think we have met, includes having an accurately dated sample that contains native microfossils, mineralogical features characteristic of life, and evidence of complex organic chemistry."

These researchers were exhaustive in their efforts to come to such conclusions. As researcher, Dr. Everett Gibson put it:

"For two years, we have applied state-of-the-art technology to perform these analyses, and we believe we have found quite reasonable evidence of past life on Mars. We don't claim that we have conclusively proven it. We are putting this evidence out to the scientific community for other investigators to verify, enhance, attack—disprove if they can—as part of the scientific process."

So just what kind of Martian meteorite are we talking about here? Well, it is an igneous (meaning volcanic-like in origin) stone, which weighs a little over four pounds. Dating of the rock shows it is just about

4.5 billion years old (about the time Earth formed). Scientists think the rock came from under the surface of Mars and that a major impact (meteor or asteroid) sent it hurtling into space. However, despite being from underground, there should have been water available to allow microbial life to form even there, just as it does on Earth.

Mind you, the fossils aren't large, being at most only about 1/100 the diameter of a human hair or even less, and with the majority being more like only 1/1000 in size. The fossils are mostly tubular looking, almost worm-like in shape with some more rounded in shape. The intriguing part of this is that these fossils amazingly, are very much like such microbial fossils also found on Earth! This fossil-bearing meteorite, referred to as ALH84001, was discovered in 1984 in Antarctica.

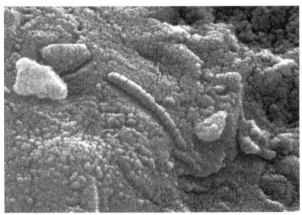

Meteorite ALH84001
Source: Public Domain

Chapter Conclusion: So what can we glean from all this information? Well, let's sort through it:

1. We have strong evidence that Mars was once much different from what it is today. There is solid evidence; some would even say incontrovertible evidence that Mars once had much more surface water than it does now.

2. This had to mean Mars had a thicker atmosphere at one point, and scientists theorize it might have been very similar to Earth's early atmosphere in which life developed here.

3. Mars, judging by the available evidence, also probably had a magnetic field to help early life survive an otherwise lethal cosmic ray bombardment.

4. These two things mean that conditions very likely were suitable for the development of life on Mars in the ancient past, just as life evolved here on Earth under such conditions.

5. Martian meteorites found here on Earth, one in particular, Meteorite ALH84001, shows real evidence of microscopic fossils. Although originally highly controversial, as to whether these were actual fossils or not, and hotly disputed as such at the time of discovery, more recent technology (since developed), does seem to indicate these probably are actual fossils. A team of leading researchers certainly thinks so, having staked their professional reputations on this idea.

Although we don't have "absolute proof" there was once life on Mars, we have ascertained there probably was. Again, there were all the right conditions on that planet early on in its development. There was a thicker atmosphere, liquid water, protection from a magnetic field, warmer environment to allow for the development of life. Moreover, we have at least one meteorite that seems definitely to show Martian fossils. This last almost constitutes, for all practical research purposes, a "smoking gun" of evidence in this regard.

Therefore, in conclusion, we can at least safely say that there quite probably was life on early Mars. The preponderance of current evidence supports this conclusion. So again, and this can't be stated too often, it would seem there was definitely once life on Mars!

However, that doesn't help us to know if there is still life on Mars today. That's the next big question and we will discuss this topic in the next chapter.

CHAPTER 5—Current Evidence For Life On Mars?

Now that we have discussed the fact that it is most likely life once may have existed on the red planet, the next question is to determine if there is life currently existing on Mars. Is there? Well, we have some tantalizing information that there just might be such evidence! First, let's remember these points:

1. Mars almost certainly has water even now. Water seems to be a prerequisite for life, and again, Mars has some water, as recently determined by our probe there.

2. Remember that Mars, at the equator, can get as high as human tolerant temperatures in the summer. This means life could survive on Mars, temperature-wise, in such conditions, just as it can here on Earth.

3. Moreover, microbes can survive an incredible range of extremely harsh conditions here on Earth. These include extreme temperature ranges as mentioned above, ones that would kill us humans in an instant, but also various degrees of salinity in water, chemical compositions in water that make them more like a toxic soup to humans, and even in the depths of the vacuum of space!

Therefore, the conditions on Mars are no worse than those extremes here on Earth in many respects. This means the extremes on Mars should be no more a barrier to certain types of microbial life than those same extremes found here on Earth. After all, microbes can live at the bottom of the ocean around volcanic vents, on the tops of the Himalayas and Antarctic, and even in boiling, toxic, mud pots in Yellowstone National Park. So why couldn't such "extremophiles," as such bacteria are called, exist on Mars? There is no reason they couldn't.

In line with that, we have some real evidence life might exist there now. NASA has been exploring Mars for some long time now. In 1976, NASA sent a couple of probes. These were the Viking probes, Vikings 1 and 2. Their purpose was to try to determine if life currently existed on Mars. To do this, the Vikings carried with them three separate means for detecting such (experiments) to try to determine the answer.

Viking 2 on Mars
Source: NASA

One of these experiments, the Labeled Release, was to become the subject of much controversy, because it actually found something in the way of evidence for life! It did this by digging up a small sample of the uppermost layer of soil. The experiment then called for the LR to add a tiny amount of water and this water had nutrients in it, as well as radioactive carbon atoms suspended in that water.

One of the first things the LR was able to determine was the soil closely resembled "veggie-garden dirt," as one source put it. In other words, the soil was very much like that which one would find in a standard vegetable garden on Earth.

The LR was designed to discover if microbial life of any sort might be in this soil. If there was such life, the theory was the Martian microbes would then "eat" (or metabolize) the nutrients in the solution and then ingest the radioactive carbon atoms in the process. This means that as a waste produce, the microbes would then give off those radioactive atoms, or alternatively, methane gas (a byproduct of such metabolism). Detectors could then measure these radioactive atoms.

This was a carefully thought out experiment, one wisely designed, because the researchers also used a number of "control" procedures to quantify and verify the results, as well. For example, the experiment also included raising the soil's temperatures to different heat levels, as well as isolating any possible microbes in darkness. This last was to cause any microbes that might have used photosynthesis to die.

What were the results? Well, they were actually astounding. The control experiments, used as a safeguard and a guarantee of sorts that any other results would be valid, all turned out to show nothing, exactly as hoped. However, the LR did show evidence of life! In addition, the results were not only positive for signs of life, but robustly so!

Neurobiologist, Joseph Miller of the University of Southern California (at the time), and once holding position of the NASA Space Shuttle Director, stated that:

"The minute the nutrients were mixed with the soil sample, you got something like 10,000 counts" of radioactive molecules—a huge spike from the 50 or 60 counts that constituted the natural background radiation on Mars."

There was one problem with all this. Despite the astounding results of the one experiment, the others did not show signs of life. Therefore, NASA, without further corroborating proof to back up the evidence simply couldn't declare there was life on Mars.

This was disheartening, of course, and so after a brief flurry of news in the press at the time, the whole experiment became forgotten. However, the story doesn't end there....

Much more recently, Doctor Miller decided, along with his researchers, to check the same data again. This time, he used a specifically designed mathematical test, a "filter" of sorts, to separate any biological results or signs from all the ones that did not contains such evidence.

The result? Doctor Miller's group said there was definite evidence of life on Mars! As he put it:

"It's very possible that if you have microbes, they're living a couple of inches beneath the soil, close to water ice."

What's more, in later missions, we have discovered that there does seem to be water just below the surface at many places on Mars, which would thus act to allow microbes to grow and multiply.

Now, just how did they arrive at this conclusion? Well, they used something known as "clustering of the data." That is, Doctor Miller and Giorgio Bianciardi, a mathematician of some renown at the University of Siena, Italy, devised a method to look for clusters of data that proved life might exist. We won't go into the details of the exact methods here. For our purposes, it is the outcome of the process and not the process itself that is of importance.

However, to explain in brief, these two men just incorporated all of the data they had. They then allowed the "cluster analysis" to proceed. The outcomes were two well-defined clusters appearing. The first cluster was the results of the LR and the second cluster contained the results of the other control experiments.

To further verify and confirm their results, they also made measurements compiled on Earth biological samples, as well as ones that weren't biological in nature. In other words, they were extremely cautious and careful to have other control procedures in place to validate any results they obtained. If there was life on Mars, it should show clusters of data similar to the experiments they did with life on Earth. What did they find? Well, as they put it:

"It turned out that all the biological experiments from Earth sorted with the active experiments from Viking, and all the nonbiological data series sorted with the control experiments. It was an extremely clear-cut phenomenon."

Their results showed life on Mars! As compelling as these results were, the research team was careful to say this wasn't absolute conclusive proof of life on Mars. However, since the outcome of the LR experiment on Mars produced incredibly similar results when compared to the Earth-based ones, there does seem to be very real evidence that life might, indeed, exist on Mars even now, and not just in the ancient past.

There is something else, as well. In prior research, Dr. Miller concluded (and published) that there seemed to be a "circadian rhythm" in the Viking experiments. Circadian rhythm is something all life, or at least, most of it seems to have in common. It is a sort of an internalized clock in life forms that govern metabolic processes. Even we humans have them and so do animals. This internal clock would include regulation of sleep time versus wake time, and temperature control within the lifeform, as well as other aspects of control over metabolic processes in living creatures.

Now the thing to remember here is that the length of a day on Mars is different from on Earth. Where our day is 24 hours, on Mars, it is just about 24.7 hours. Doctor Miller discovered that the LR showed that measurements of radiation in the experiment altered, and this alteration coincided with various times of the Martian day, the longer day than ours is on Earth. As he put it in his conclusions:

"If you look closely, you could see that the [radioactive-gas measurement] was going up during the day and coming down at night. ... The oscillations had a period of 24.66 hours just about on the nose. That is basically a circadian rhythm, and we think circadian rhythms are a good signal for life."

This then acts as more evidence for their being life on Mars right now!

There is one odd note about all this. Doctor Miller felt that until people could actually see microbes in a petri dish, living ones, they would not be finally convinced that life existed on Mars. This would be relatively simple for NASA to do on one of its missions.

Yet despite all this tantalizing evidence, NASA has never done so! The question is, why? Why haven't they done something so simple if only in order to finally prove or disprove there is life on Mars? As Doctor Miller put it:

"...for some reason, NASA has never flown a microscope that would let you do something like that. If they can fly a microscope for the geologists, they should be able to fly one for the biologists."

Yet, NASA has not done this so far. Again, it makes one wonder why.

Methane. Methane, a gas, has been found on Mars. Now perhaps the most common source on Earth for Methane is as a byproduct, or waste products of living organisms. This means there could well be microbial life on mars generating this methane.

There are several other ways possible to generate methane, as well, but these are much less common and the main one of these requires atmospheric water chemically to combine with surface material, salts, also known as "perchlorates" to release methane. The problem with this is that we see very little water vapor in the atmosphere of Mars and even less of it at lower altitudes (near the surface) to cause this reaction. This, by the way, is only a hypothesis for Mars and not even on the level of a theory yet.

The other possibility for methane production might be a venting that the Curiosity Rover detected. This means there could have been a chance outgassing of methane from an underground site on the planet. If so, this would have been a remarkable coincidence for it to encounter such a rare event, the Rover being there just when this happened. Since there isn't much methane on Mars, such venting should be rare occurrences, so again, Rover sort of "tripping over" such an event should have been greatly against the odds.

Again, the most probable explanation for methane on Earth (when encountered) is that it is the result of organic (life) metabolizing. Therefore, it is reasonable to assume it may have the same cause on Mars.

Does methane act as a smoking gun for life on the red planet? Not quite, but it adds to the general body of evidence and in the process, keeps increasing the validity of the idea that there is actual life on Mars now. Otherwise, what is the source of the methane?

NASA's Mars rover Curiosity found methane
Source: NASA/JPL

Chapter Conclusion: Mars might have extreme conditions for life by our standards here on Earth, but as we have discovered in recent times, a class of organisms grouped as "extremophiles" do live under such harsh and unfriendly conditions right here on our planet. They exist, as mentioned earlier, in the depths of oceans everywhere, including around super-heated water from volcanic vents. They exist on high mountaintops, and in the polar regions of our Earth. Microbes exist for long periods when exposed to the vacuum of space and the attendant deadly radiation of our sun there, along with cosmic radiation, and incredible extremes of temperature. This means that there are forms of microbial life that could certainly live in certain areas of Mars where the conditions, at present, would allow them to thrive.

Then there is the matter of methane detected on Mars. This gas is a result of organic matter in most cases, and so this further lends support to the idea there is currently life on the red planet.

Moreover, the LR experiment showed life on Mars, as well. What's more, recent analysis of the same data again further supports the idea there is life there.

So is there? Is there life on Mars? Well, it would seem more likely than not, that life, at least on the microbial level, might well exist there. The probability is high. In short, if one had to bet on life being there, if you wanted to win that bet, you'd better go with the idea that life, indeed, exists on Mars right now, at least on the microbial level.

This is interesting, but let's be honest here; most of us, although excited at the idea that life might exist on a nearby planet, or anywhere else in the universe for that matter, really want to know if there is intelligent life there.

What of life that is intelligent? What of Martians or aliens? Do they exist? Can they exist on Mars? Is their evidence for such a thing being real? In the following chapters, we will discuss this.

PART III—MARTIANS OR EXTRATERRESTRIALS ON MARS?

CHAPTER 6—Evidence Of Intelligent Life On Mars.

Now we come to the most burning question of all, or at least, certainly the most popular one:

Is there intelligent life on Mars? This question has concerned and consumed humanity's interest for centuries now. So, again, is there intelligent life on Mars?

The quick answer to that is no, there is nothing of the sort there, because the planet is too inhospitable for complex living creatures to exist. At least, this is what NASA and other scientists are saying right now and want us to believe.

Are they right? Maybe, but then they have been wrong so often about things in the past relating to Mars, such as about Mars having no water, haven't they? Perhaps they are this time, as well, as we shall see just might be the case.

Again, is there evidence for life on Mars and if so, what kind of evidence is there? Let's start with the idea there might once have been intelligent life, but now there is no longer (and yes, we will discuss the possibility of intelligent life perhaps existing there now, as well, later on).

What types of evidence might support the idea of sentient (intelligent) beings having once occupied the red planet. Well, physical evidence of ruins and such would certainly supply irrefutable evidence of such a thing. Since we have little (other than the two Rovers) on Mars actually and physically reconnoitering the planet, we have to fall back to photographs of the surface of Mars, taken from space, and on the data supplied from the ground from the Rovers.

With regard to the satellites, there are currently 14 known Earth-origin satellites in orbit around Mars. Those still active and sending signals include:

Mars Odyssey, of the United States, NASA launched April 7, 2001.

Mars Express of the European Space Agency ESA launched June 2, 2003.

Mars Reconnaissance Orbiter, of the United States, NASA launched August 12, 2005.

Mangalyaan, of India, the ISRO, launched November 5, 2013.

MAVEN, of the United States, NASA launched November 18, 2013.

ExoMars Trace Gas Orbiter. European Space Agency, launched March 14, 2016.

As mentioned earlier, these "lucky ones" made it to Mars, seeming to have avoided the curse of other probes launched to there. These satellites managed to enter orbit around the planet, and still managed to go on functioning. Moreover, these satellites are capable of high-resolution pictures of the Martian surface. Furthermore, they have different kinds of cameras, using different types of light wavelengths, such as infrared, etc. This means that although we do not have much on the surface of Mars to see things up close, other than NASA's brave little Rovers, we are getting very high quality pictures from near Mars orbit of the surface.

Are any of those pictures evidence for intelligent life having once existed on Mars? Well, it could well be they are, and these photos would come from both the orbiters, as well as the Rovers on the Martian surface. Below, are some of the more interesting ones, but not all of the photographs that seem to show something are included here. There simply isn't room here for so many, and yes, there are that many!

However, one has to view these with a critical eye. The reason for this is a phenomenon most of us are familiar with (if not the name of it), that causes us to see "things," such as objects and/or patterns in images that aren't really there. This phenomenon is known as Pareidolia, and as Wikipedia describes it:

"...is a psychological phenomenon in which the mind responds to a stimulus, usually an image or a sound, by perceiving a familiar pattern where none exists..."

In other words, it is the same sort of thing as seeing a face in the random pattern of a ceramic tile, or an animal in a cloud formation. The human mind tries to "see" things, to make sense out of that which is random by searching for patterns that mean something to us.

So keeping this caveat in mind, let's look at some of the photos taken. What one looks for in these pictures is anything different that doesn't look natural, but rather artificially made. In other words, we look for something too artificial looking to be something that might have come about by chance through erosion, weathering of any sort, geological activity, etc. Now, let's get started:

1. Strange dome-like structure. A satellite photo of a dome and one by the Opportunity Rover—shows images of what appear to be dome-like structures.

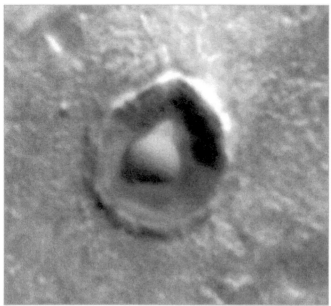

Dome-like structure in Crater
Source: NASA

Domes?
Source: NASA, Opportunity Rover

Notice in the top photo that the "dome" almost has a geodesic dome look to it and appears very round, and smoothly so, too smoothly so, in fact. Is this a natural phenomenon or a result of Pareidolia? You decide. For me, it has an artificial look to it and judging solely by the image, appears too artificial to have been made by "natural causes."

In the photograph immediately above this paragraph, the one taken by the Opportunity Rover, there seem to be two sorts of domes. There is a large one on the left that appears smooth. In fact, it is so smooth it is causing sunlight to reflect off the near side of it, as if it were metallic or polished ceramic in nature.

Again, this looks artificial to me, because nothing like it has been seen on Earth that isn't artificial in nature. Notice the evenly spaced dark areas around the base of the dome, as if being some sort of windows or entranceways into the structure. If these are just rocks in the foreground, they certainly are regularly spaced and shaped much the same. Could it be natural? Possibly, but if I had to bet on it, I'd say the dome was artificial, not natural. Again, you must decide for yourself.

To the right is another structure that also appears "dome-like" but of a different shape and size. Again, notice the regular dark areas (windows?) spaced around it about a third of the way down from the top. The large dome on the left has the same sort of thing down near the visible portion of its base. If these are natural and not artificial, how do we account for the difference in the weathering processes that put one set of dark areas high up on the more narrow dome, but around the base of the larger one? Also, how did they become so smooth and shiny, as to look metallic, when nothing else around them has done the same? These domes stick out like the proverbial "thumb" in the landscape, and this adds to the idea they must be artificial and so intelligently made.

There is also something in the foreground and "s-shaped" in design, something that might be a tube of sorts, or even a cleared path or road area. Again, are these natural objects or the result of our minds playing tricks on us?

I will say this: they definitely don't look natural, not to me. Again, you must decide for yourself. By the way, these are unretouched photos (except for a bit of sharpening of the image by me to clarify what one is seeing), and so to claim they are hoaxes just doesn't fly. You can see the photos for yourself by going to the link listed in the References section at the end of this book.

2. Infrared photo of an underground city? In this infrared photo, there is what appears to be a grid-like pattern of a subterranean or buried city, or at least, the ruins of such:

Source: Fobos 2, Russian Mission

Enterprise Mission, Thermal Scan of same region 13 Years later.
Source: NASA

Thermal (Infrared) Image of "Something"
On Mars, Canadian Television
Source: Phobos 2 Mission

Now, to get an idea of the scale of these images, I must mention that Dr. John Becklake of the London Science Museum said:

"The city-like pattern **[first photograph in this group]** *is 60 kilometers wide and could be easily be mistaken for an aerial view of Los Angeles."*

Furthermore, the area photographed was approximately 230 square miles, or 595.697 square kilometers. Notice the rectangular pattern, the numerous straight lines, some being thin, and some being wider, but most being just about the same, just as roads in one of our major cities on Earth would have. Is this an ancient buried city on Mars?

As the saying goes, "nature abhors straight lines," and these lines are definitely straight, so are they artificial? Moreover, how did a "grid-like" pattern come to be just below the surface of Mars?

What is even odder about the images is that something there was giving off heat. Remember, this is an infrared photo, otherwise known as "thermal imaging," and a type used to take photographs that show heat sources.

Why did a camera designed to take pictures of things giving off heat have this underground grid work show up on it, unless it was radiating some type of heat? The heat source would have to be either natural, as in underground volcanic activity, or artificial. Chances are, if this is an artificial source of heat, it would have to be radioactive in origin. That leads to even something more tantalizing about Mars, which we will consider in a later chapter. Even so, another photo (second photograph down in this group), shows the pattern is still there when another thermal imaging photograph was taken of the region some 13 years later! So the heat goes on!

3. Tracks on Mars. Now we come to a truly odd image. This one showed a possible landing site (one of several) for probes to land, and the strange thing about this photo is that there are definite straight-line tracks clearly visible across the surface. What is even more bizarre is that these supposedly could not be of human origin, since no human craft ever landed in this region.

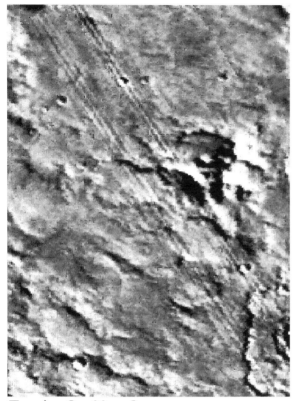

Tracks On Mars?
Source: NASA

These tracks, these multiple parallel straight lines, and they are VERY straight, have a large space between them. What's more, it is difficult to be sure if they go "over" everything, or if some things occurred after the tracks were somehow laid down.

However, the tracks do seem to go over most of the craters, so they had to have appeared there after the craters came to be. Yet if one looks down at the very bottom right corner of the picture, one can see where the tracks come to a ridge. They do appear to go over the ridge and through what appears to be a crater (very bottom right of photograph) and then on. However, just slightly higher and to the left of the ridge is what appears to be a circular crater. The "left track" stops here. This means this impact crater had to have occurred after the tracks appeared on the surface, since they disappeared at this point. So although the tracks are relatively young, as compared to the other craters, they have to be old enough to have suffered obliteration by the impact creating the one crater, at least. This means that although the tracks are old, they are not "incredibly ancient."

4. Statues on Mars? These following photos probably belong in the classification of "in the eye of the beholder," but here are some photos that do draw our interest as researchers, as well:

"Woman On Mars," Curiosity Rover
Source: NASA

This picture raised many questions when it hit the Internet. It seems to show a figure of a woman standing atop an outcropping of rock in roughly the center of the photograph. However, I doubt seriously if this is a statue of a woman, myself.

For instance, one can see a rill, or course line in the sand that runs right through her as it goes from bottom left to upper right "behind her" diagonally up the picture. Therefore, whatever this is, it can't be something solid. More likely (in my opinion), it is either shadow of some sort, or even something flowing (water?) down the hillside. Still, many find this photo very intriguing. In fact, even I do. It really does rather resemble a woman standing on a rock. What do you think? Is it a woman, or just an illusion? Again, in my opinion it is not a woman. Anyway, here is another:

Statue on mars? Or just a very strange
 Rock Formation?
Source: NASA

This picture definitely looks like something "solid." Yes, it does look like a statue of someone kneeling, perhaps in an act of supplication at first glance, but look closer. The extension of the out-stretched arm is not as complete as it first appears. A rill in the ground behind the "statue" actually completes the look of the outstretched arm, but notice that particular portion of the arm is the same color as the soil behind the "statue." Still, even if the arm isn't complete, the thing does resemble a human or alien figure of sorts, one kneeling. Yet, there is another problem. Look at the surrounding darker rock material, the outcrops. They are the same coloration. So if it is a statue, it was carved from the same native material as those other rock outcrops were. Yet, it is still intriguing. Even without the arm completed, it is such an odd shape. Again, I leave it to the reader to decide. Here is another photograph that has excited interest:

Monolith On Mars?
Source: NASA

This one is of more interest to me, because it shows what appears to be a rectangular monolith jutting well above the surrounding terrain. One can see this by the length of the shadow it is casting compared to the surrounding outcrops. Therefore, this is definitely an anomalous thing, not consistent with the immediate environment.

What is the monolith doing there? Why is it so different in size and shape from all the other surrounding material? Since it is unlikely that the monolith just eroded into this shape "in situ" in this particular place, since nothing nearby looks anything like it, it had to have "landed" there, as some form of ejecta from the impact of a meteorite, or it is artificial in nature.

Yes, it could be a form of ejecta, but the rectangular nature of the thing is not the normal shape for such types of things here on Earth, and we can only assume the laws of physics with regard to this sort of thing work the same way on Mars....

5. **Glass Tubes?** One of most unusual photographs taken are what appear to be long and large glass tubes, or as one person put it "worms." They have what look to be supporting arches built into them and strongly resemble some sort of transparent transportation tube of some type.

However, they could be for just about anything, including the channeling of water without loss or evaporation to the thin and dry atmosphere, for instance, and this is assuming they are artificial in nature. Some argue these may be a natural phenomenon, similar to lava tubes, and yet they look nothing like lava tubes we've seen here on Earth.

Two researchers were so impressed with the images that they referred to them as:

"...the real smoking gun as to life on Mars."

Personally, I wouldn't go that far, but the image is real and in its unretouched state looks exactly like how some researchers have described it, as being some sort of glass tubes or translucent material, partially uncovered, or running through aboveground areas at different points, perhaps. Malin Space Science Systems posted this image in June of 2000, and of course, have raised an enormous amount of controversy as a result.

As pointed out by some researchers, the tubes look to be in excellent shape and don't seem to have undergone the extreme weathering or eroding that other anomalies (whether forts, statues, ruins, etc.) on Mars have undergone. Moreover, this is the only image (so far) of Mars that shows such translucent tubes. The ridges or arches are roughly regularly spaced, which also makes the structure look even more artificial in nature and not natural. In fact, just what the tubes are, is a complete mystery. As famous writer, Arthur C. Clarke, put it:

"I'm still waiting for an explanation of that extraordinary glass worm on... **[Mars]***... How big is it? It's one of the most incredible images that's ever come from space and there have been no comments on it whatsoever!"*

Well, maybe there were no comments on it at the time, but that has since changed. This photograph has gone viral among researchers since then.

What are the "glass" tubes exactly? Well, at this point, nobody seems to know or even to be able to come up with a reasonable explanation for the thing. As of now, it's just another anomaly, a very bizarre one, indeed, on the red planet. For all we know, it could be something that was once living and is now fossilized:

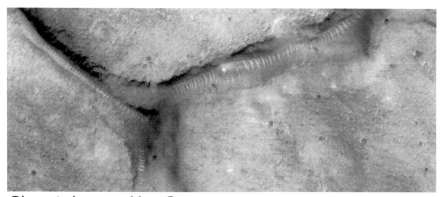

Glass tubes on Mars?
Sources: NASA/JPL via Malin Space Science Systems

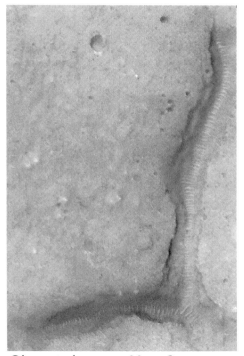

Glass tubes on Mars?
Sources: NASA/JPL via Malin Space Science Systems

There are a few points more to consider about these images. That these tubes appear to be of a translucent nature, or at least glass-like is not in question. Their high reflectivity, "smooth as glass" exteriors all make the tubes seem this way. However, I question the idea they were some sort of transportation system, since they seem to narrow and trail off at the ends. The apparent misshaped portions, ones that seem wider than others, could well just be the way they are showing, having once been underground, perhaps. This would mean the soil in some areas, eroded away more than in others, or blew away more during the frequent dust storms that plague Mars and so just give the appearance of irregular shapes to the tubes.

Even so, they do appear to be "naturally" uneven to me, being narrower at points, and wider at others. Again, whatever they are, they are also a mystery yet to be solved.

There are numerous other photos such as these of anomalies on Mars. Some show what look to be pyramids, others show all sorts of things, including, of course, the infamous "face on Mars" which I deliberately did not include here.

First, everyone who has any interest in Mars research has seen these photos by now, since they've been all over the Internet and on the media before that. Secondly, I have doubts as to whether the "face" is a real artifact in the sense of being artificial. It could just be a trick of the lighting in the photograph making us see a face there.

However, there are a number of pyramid-shaped formations very close to the face, so it does make one wonder… In any case, photos of bizarre objects on Mars are numerous, and depending on their clarity, can be either construed as just wish fulfillment on the part of the beholder, but in some cases, do seem to show "something" very odd, such as the domes. There simply isn't room for them all in this book. Please check the "References" section for links to such pictures.

Chapter Conclusion: Although there is still no "smoking gun" to prove intelligent life once existed on Mars, there does seem to be some photographic evidence of some very "anomalous" features as scientists insist upon calling them. Most convincing for me are the dome pictures, as well as the tracks image, among others.

Do they prove life existed on Mars? No, they do not, but they are tantalizing evidence that helps support the idea. The tracks for instance, simply cannot be logically accounted for virtually any other way. Some theories proposed by various researchers as to how they are "naturally" produced are so "out there," that if one uses the Principle of Occam's Razor, a tool used by most scientists; one has to take the far simpler explanation: that is, they are artificial in nature and not natural. Therefore, they could well be the result of intelligent life. Judging by the destruction of a portion of the tracks by an impact crater, they must be relatively old.

Furthermore, in the next chapters, we will see there are other types of evidence that indicate there might, indeed, have been intelligent life on Mars, and what's more, some form of intelligent life might still exist there now.

CHAPTER 7—How Did Intelligent Life End On Mars?

If we can accept the idea that there indeed, might have been intelligent life on Mars at one time, then we have to consider how it might have ended. This too would constitute evidence for intelligent life in itself, because if the ending was not natural, that, too, shows intelligent minds were behind what ultimately happened.

First, there are a number of theories about Mars, why it is no longer a wet and warmer world. In addition, yes, we are sure now that the red planet once had oceans, a thicker atmosphere, and was considerably warmer than it is now, as mentioned earlier. How do we know this? There are a number of ways. One that is very hard to refute is the type of rock that makes up regions of Mars. The three main types of rock we know of here on Earth are igneous, metamorphic, and sedimentary.

Don't let those terms bother you, they just mean that one type of rock is volcanic in origin (igneous), one is the result of silt being deposited in various layers in water, as with sea beds, which build up in layers and over time become hardened, as in sandstone, claystone, and mudstone, as well as other types of sedimentary rock. The third type is where rock, such as sedimentary stone, is compressed and reworked in a planet's crust.

With tremendous pressures and heat applied, the sedimentary stone undergoes a major transformation. This typically creates a much harder rock and because of the time involved in the process, makes for very old rock, or stone that dates back a long ways in origin, since such transformations take a lot of time. The layers of sedimentary stone have to be buried, altered slowly over the ages, and then must be thrust up, or until the surface erodes down to reveal them once more.

One of the things we do know about Mars is there does seem to be all these sorts of stone, including sedimentary. In fact, there seems to be quite a lot of sedimentary rock. So much so, in fact, that we can conclude that since such stone was laid down in water originally, there had to be lots of water and for quite some time in order for this to take place.

With that much water, the atmosphere would be much thicker (water vapor is a greenhouse gas), and so the planet would trap more heat and thus be warmer. Immediately below this paragraph, please find a picture of a Martian landscape. Clearly, anyone can see layers of sediment showing in the surrounding hills there. Again, sedimentary means there was enough water to create such rock layers:

Martian Landscape, Mt. Sharp, layers of rock showing due to erosion
Source: NASA, Curiosity Rover

Since different layers of sedimentary rock can have different thicknesses and hardness, depending on the material laid down to make them, some of the softer layers in between erode faster, leaving the harder layers sticking out, as in the above photo. Moreover, there are some types of minerals that can only be created with water present. Scientists have strong evidence for these types of minerals being on Mars, as well.

What does this mean? Again, it means there was water and a good amount of it, as well as a resulting thicker atmosphere, and even a magnetic field to help keep it from being blown away by solar radiation. We have real evidence for such a magnetic field, by the way, in the form of magnetized rocks on Mars.

What happened to all the water and atmosphere? Well, there are a number of theories.

1. A cold and small planet. Mars is a good deal farther out from the sun than we are. Despite its warm start, this theory says the planet was simply too small to have plate tectonics (continental drift) as we have here on Earth. The planet, being small, also cooled much more rapidly than our world.

Without constant volcanic activity, the atmosphere wasn't replenished as ours is by outgassing. Moreover, being farther out from the sun, it became colder much more swiftly. Therefore, a lot of the water moisture locked up into ice. The planet chilled further without the water vapor in the atmosphere acting as a greenhouse gas, and of course, the atmosphere became thinner without the water vapor. With the death of the magnetic field, solar radiation started blowing away the atmosphere, as well.

Again, being a small world, one with much less gravity than on Earth, nothing stopped this process, which became a vicious downward spiral. The planet became colder, dryer as even the surface ice began to undergo a process called sublimation. If you've ever noticed that snowbanks shrink on a very dry day, even though the temperature is still well below freezing, that's sublimation. The snow changes to water vapor directly without first melting to water.

Furthermore, the planet's crust would have quakes as it chilled, shrunk, and compressed. This is one of the main theories of how that giant canyon, the Valles Marineris, came to be. Yet, that theory of the canyon's origin has largely been discounted. In any case, Mars was a failed experiment for life and died with a whimper instead of a "bang," at least, as some scientists theorize.

There are problems with this theory. For one thing, it doesn't seem to allow enough time for all that sedimentary rock and minerals to have formed on Mars. The theory indicates that the planet should have not only rapidly lost its water vapor, but the water still there on the surface would have been in the form of ice fairly early on, as well, and so not allowing for the rock to form as it seems to have. No water, no silt to sift down and create layers of stone. There are other problems with the theory, as well, but let's move on.

2. Asteroid Impact. Another theory is that a huge impact, quite possibly an asteroid from the Asteroid Belt struck the planet and so sounded its death knell. The impact would have been huge. According to various sources, including *Scientific American* Magazine, such a collision would have almost shattered the planet. In fact, such an impact would have been incredibly "violent" and more so "than was previously imagined." The asteroid striking Mars would have caused half the surface of that world to melt.

This idea by scientists comes from something known as "the Martian hemispheric dichotomy." The planet is almost in two unequal halves in a sense. The bottom or southern half (south of the equator) of Mars is much higher overall (generally), in altitude. The southern half of Mars, on average, is about 5.5 kilometers higher than north of the equator! This is a significant difference in altitude! Moreover, the fact the planet is so evenly divided this way is striking.

Where scientists once thought an asteroid might have delivered a sideswipe to the north pole of Mars, this new study, in *Geophysical Research Letters*, showed that it was more likely a huge impact that struck south of the equator. Computer simulations showed that such an impact would have melted the surface rock of mars, caused it to flow, and thus accounting for the differences between the northern regions where it didn't directly hit, and the southern regions where it did.

Furthermore, the impact would have caused two giant tsunamis, sometimes still called tidal waves. The first would have been as the asteroid penetrated the Martian sea(s), forcing a huge wall of water out and away from the impact point in all directions. The second wave would have been generated as the asteroid then went on to crash into the crust of Mars. Furthermore, much of the water on the planet at the time would have vaporized and simply then been lost to space, so superheated was it.

Finally, because of the intense explosion, the convection of magma below the Martian surface would have been utterly disrupted. The Martian magnetic field would have died. Nor would it have renewed itself after things had settled down. Once "switched off," as one researcher put it, the magnetic field, a weak one to begin with, would never have returned. The atmosphere of Mars, what was left of it, would then begin to blow away over time, driven from the small planet's weak gravitational clutches by solar winds from our sun.

There are problems with this theory, too. For one thing, this impact had to have come late in the planet's history to allow sedimentary layers to develop, and such giant impacts would be exceedingly rare, most having already occurred early on in the formation of the solar system.

Even then, such events would have been rare, and so this impact would seem to have occurred early on in the development of Mars. Yet, it couldn't have. Again, the formation of rocks, sedimentary and otherwise, that simply need a great deal of time under relatively stable conditions to form did take place. So where did this monster asteroid come from, when, and why?

Moreover, the simulation calls for an impact of an asteroid that would have been larger than Earth's Moon, being some 4,000 kilometers in diameter. This, too, seems highly unlikely, because the Moon is big. Where was it hiding in our solar system to intersect with the orbit of Mars?

Furthermore, rather than such tiny moons as Phobos and Deimos, the impact theoretically should have hurled massive amounts of material into space, as happened with Earth's supposed impact with the theorized planet Theia early in its history. Mars should thus have a bigger moon or moons by far, just as Earth has a bigger moon. However, Mars does not. If all the material fell back onto the planet, why do we not see evidence of this in the northern hemisphere, as well? There should have been an incredible bombardment. Endless numbers of craters, but we do not see any sign of this.

Finally, the theory does not explain the formation of the vast Valles Marineris Canyon, that massive, United States-wide canyon with its incredible depths. Something must account for that tremendous geologically feature, but just what?

The theory does account for how Mars might have lost much of its early atmosphere. Such an impact would have been devastating to any major bodies of water on the planet, undoubtedly. The rest, as they say, would have been "history." Still, it doesn't explain other things. Well, there is another theory that could very well account for such things and we will discuss this in the next chapter.

Chapter Conclusion: These theories are two of the most prominent ones on the death of Mars as a warm wet world. They both have things that fit well with what we see on Mars today, but they also have major problems, as well. They simply don't account for everything we see there on Mars now.

Therefore, it may be that neither theory is right or at least entirely right and so would need major modifications. Moreover, there is a third theory, and one that accredited scientists and researchers have been checking into.....

CHAPTER 8—A War On Mars?

Mars destroyed by war. Bona fide researchers and not just conspiracy theorists, unbelievably, have proposed this theory, that Mars died because of a major war. Besides, it accounts for much that the other theories of the death of a warm wet Mars simply do not, including the formation of the Martian Grand Canyon. So, exactly, what is the theory?

Well, Dr. John Brandenburg, a physicist who has worked extensively in the field of plasmas, first proposed the idea as a real scientific theory. He thinks that ancient Mars had an advanced civilization and a nuclear holocaust destroyed it.

Additionally, he thinks, and this is an incredible idea, that the nuclear war came from elsewhere, another race of aliens attacking the Martians. In his theory, Martians, or as he calls them, Cydonians and Utopians (two separate races?), named for regions of Mars where we see what look like ruins, were wiped out and the results of that attack are still there on Mars, plain for all of us to see, if we only view them in the right way.

Now, as bizarre as all this seems to be, it must be remembered Dr. Brandenburg had impeccable credentials prior to his proposing this theory. As mentioned, he has done considerable work in the field of plasma physics. In fact, his degree, a PhD from the University of California at Davis, is for Theoretical Plasma Physics. This in itself is no small achievement. At the writing of this book, Dr. Brandenburg held a position at Orbital Technologies as a plasma physicist, as well. Furthermore, he has authored a number of books. In short, when it comes to how plasmas behave, how they act, and the evidence they leave behind, he is an expert.

Because of his solid background and impeccable work experience, he has a thorough knowledge of plasma being used for weaponry purposes, as well as having dealt with such subjects as varying theoretical types of propulsion methods. Moreover, his having been consulted on directed energy weapons, as well, is common knowledge. So exactly what is Dr. Brandenburg's theory about what happened on Mars? Well, he believes:

1. Two massive nuclear explosions. At some time in the past, two vast explosions took place on Mars, definitely nuclear ones. He claims there is evidence for this. He cites the fact there is evidence of radioactive material all over Mars for such a nuclear holocaust, forming a thin layer on the planet's surface, as well as in the atmosphere. This material includes radioactive potassium, thorium, and uranium. What's more, this radioactive material is centered on a "hot spot," meaning the blast site as he believes, is the original source of it all. He further indicates that the reddish coloration of the surface of Mars is due to the blasts.

2. Nuclear isotopes in Martian atmosphere. As further evidence for his theory, he points to the fact there are nuclear isotopes, ones associated with fusion reactions, such as hydrogen thermonuclear blasts would produce. This, for him, acts as a powerful indicator that leads him to believe the bombs came from space.

He refers to the fact that there is Xenon-129, a radioactive isotope, *"in high concentration."* Other scientists refute this part of his theory saying that such products can be the result of natural processes, referring to the idea of a naturally occurring georeactor type of explosion, where there just happens to be enough nuclear material in a region to trigger a natural atomic explosion of such a kind.

Originally, Dr. Brandenburg had thought there might have been a natural georeactor-type of nuclear explosion, as well, but as his theory developed, he ruled this idea out is impractical. He believes the evidence just doesn't fit such a scenario.

3. Location of blasts. It is Dr. Brandenburg's contention that the region of Cydonia on Mars was the probable location of one of the nuclear blasts. He hypothesizes that one center of civilization was there and the other, a smaller center, was at Galaxias Chaos, another region.

4. Type of ancient civilization. Brandenburg believes there was an ancient civilization on Mars, a well-advanced one, perhaps on a par with some of our own ancient civilizations, such as Egypt, Babylon, or others. Therefore, as Dr. Brandenburg puts it:

"Taken together, the data requires that the hypothesis of Mars as the site of an ancient planetary nuclear massacre must now be considered."

He further says that what happened on Mars just might explain the so-called Fermi Paradox, where a famous scientist, Dr. Fermi, wondered why in a universe full of stars and planets, why humans had yet to receive any sign or signal that other intelligent lifeforms exist "out there." Dr. Brandenburg feels they just might be killed off by some evil spacefaring alien race that for some reason doesn't want other intelligent species to exist. Perhaps, this is a form of survival of the fittest on their part, an interspecies competition for survival. If this is the case, then Earth might be in danger, as well. As he said:

"Providentially, we are forewarned of this possible aspect of the cosmos."

He is not alone in this belief. Other famous scientists have echoed this fear. This includes no less than Stephen Hawking himself, the internationally renowned physicist and author. Nor is Dr. Brandenburg the first to suggest nuclear war, or some kind of war, may have raged at some time in our solar system. Others have promoted this scenario, as well.

5. Martian atmosphere destroyed. Because of how small a planet Mars is, Dr. Brandenburg proposed the idea that two such massive hydrogen thermonuclear explosions would have been sufficient to blast much of the Martian atmosphere into space. The planet then would be left as a dying world with little air left.

6. Ancient texts on earth. Ancient Vedic texts of India/Pakistan speak of a great war waged by "demons" or aliens in space and with a large number of different types of aliens involved. The Mahabharata, and to a lesser extent, the Ramayana Codices speak of battles waged in space around Earth, in our solar system, and even one battle that took place on the Moon.

Sumerian cuneiform writings also speak of a race from the heavens that once controlled Earth, the Anunnaki, who created humans as a slave race, and then afterwards at some point, had to fight a major war. During that war, humans rose up in rebellion, as well, against their alien masters. Ultimately, the aliens retreated from Earth, but whether this was a result of the human rebellion against them, losing the war in space, or both, is uncertain.

Although we may see such tales as fanciful legends and myths, the Indian Hindus did not. They regard it as their legitimate ancient history, pure and simple, even as the Sumerian culture did, as well. So true or not, history or legend—it all seems to be in the eye of the beholder.

Yet, the Sumerians and ancient Indians were not alone in these so-called legends. Even Native North and South Americans, various tribes of them, have tales that speak of such things. If this is all just a myth or a legend, then it is certainly a worldwide one. Yes, the stories do vary in details, as such things will, but overall, the tales are surprisingly consistent, even so. In addition, they are highly coincidental, as well.

Approximate Locations of Centers of Nuclear Explosions

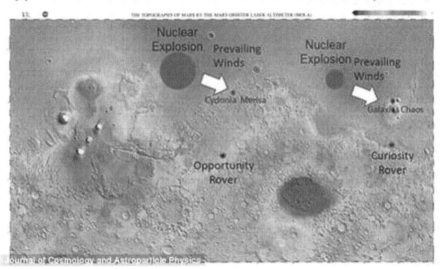

Credit Source: Daily Mail, United Kingdom, Journal of Cosmology And Astroparticle Physics
Source: Public Domain

Plasma weapons attack Mars. There is also considerable controversy about the Valles Marineris, that giant Grand Canyon of Mars. There are those that argue it was not the result of the planet cooling (an idea that is now being discounted by many mainstream researchers in any case), but the result of some catastrophic war on Mars.

They point to the fact that on Earth there are no surviving rocks from the time of the Earth's formation.

Recycling of the Earth's crust, erosion, etc., have combined to destroy the original stone that formed on our planet. What we do have are some very old types of rock, including some found on the island of Tasmania, Australia, and some in the Canadian Precambrian Shield. However, again, these are not the stone formed at the time of the Earth's formation, but came later.

Therefore, some researchers say that the idea that the Valles Marineris could date back to the origins of Mars, be the result of that planet's crust cooling and shrinking and still be there in such pristine shape seems highly unlikely. Erosion, those Martian seas, early Martian rivers, floods, landslides, huge dust storms, and such should all have combined to fade the canyon into oblivion, or at least soften and hide many of the features we see there today.

The fact the canyon is still there in such graphic relief and detail would seem to be contrary to what many geologists would expect after billions or even millions of years. Again, time and weathering should have taken its toll and obliterated the canyon long ago. That is, if indeed it was ever so old to begin with. These same researchers say the canyon must have formed differently and not so long ago as four billion years. Dr. Brandenburg thinks the canyon's formation had to have been much more recently.

Because of some oddities about the canyon, others argue a weapon of mass destruction of some sort might have caused the creation of the huge gash in the landscape of Mars. They point to the fact the Canyon does not seem to be the result of either erosion by water, or again, of crustal shrinkage because of the shape and form of it.

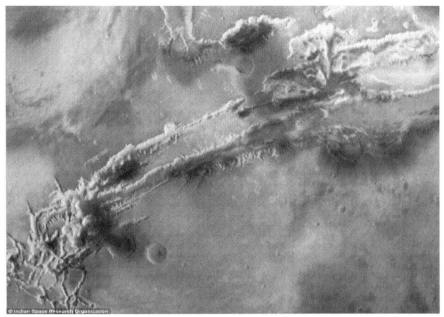

Valles Marineris as seen from India's Orbiter
Source: Indian Space Research Organization

The proponents of this theory say the canyon looks almost exactly like what is produced when lightning strikes soil or sand, as in the images below, although on a far greater scale on Mars, of course:

Lightning Fulgurite (fused sand)
Source: Public Domain

Lightning Striking Concrete
Image Public Domain

Lightning Striking Concrete, with results similar to the look Of the Valles Marineris.
Image: Public Domain

Such researchers have a point. There is a marked similarity to gashes caused by lightning (and the plasma created by lightning) with the appearance of Valles Marineris. If the Grand Canyon of Mars wasn't created by erosion, as most exogeologists now hypothesize, and if the idea that it was created by crustal shrinkage due to cooling has too many problems to hold up, then such a massive plasma discharge, and it would have to have been a truly massive one, might have caused such a phenomenon.

Again, one has to admit the images above, although miniature versions compared to the mighty Valles Marineris, do look amazing similar in nature, if not scope. They are complete with the long jagged lines, the deep gash areas, and the odd way it plays across the landscape.

Some of these same researchers argue the creation of the canyon may have somehow been natural, as with a massive plasma discharge from the sun, or just an electrical buildup between the planets that might somehow discharge (see, Electric Universe Theory). These researchers argue the early solar system had much debris in it, an incredible amount, and that this debris, protoplanets by the hundreds or even thousands, asteroids, meteorites, comets, dust, gasses, etc., might have built up powerful charges from the sun's radiation.

This idea is not as fanciful as it may seem. Planets often, at least early on, do possess powerful charges due to their magnetic fields, ones created by spinning cores and convection flows in their magma. Anyone who watches a powerful thunderstorm on Earth can see the strong charges that can build up. These same researchers say the early solar system might have been much more powerful in this respect, with regard to electrical charges and/or plasma charges (superheated charged gases) could have been common back then. The dust and other debris in the solar system could have acted as a sort of "electrical conduit" for such giant discharges to take. The proponents of the Electric Universe Theory think that perhaps incredibly powerful discharges between planets occurred at times, and that the Valles Marineris on Mars was one of the consequences of such a massive discharge.

This theory does not contravene what we know about electrical charges and plasma. In fact, these theories are an outgrowth of the knowledge we've gained in recent decades in this matter. Furthermore, they point to the fact that ancient history texts describe such mighty charges or "bolts" and that almost all cultures talk about them in their verbal legends.

Still, there is a problem with this theory, too. That is, the same one as the idea the canyon formed from the shrinkage of the Martian crust. It would have happened just too long ago for there still to be evidence of such a mighty discharge. Surely, erosion, weathering, and obfuscating sandstorms and landslides (as well as water acting to erode the canyon) would have done much to do away with the Valles Marineris long ago.

We don't have such massive electrical discharges between planets now, and we've seen no evidence of anything like that for as long as we've been observing the heavens. Therefore, such discharges had to have occurred, even if they occurred at all, a long time ago when the solar system was much younger. If so, then evidence for them in the form of Valles Marineris should have long since disappeared, eroded away, even as the originally rock and stone on early Earth has been "recycled."

In any case, Dr. Brandenburg believes there were to nuclear explosions, massive ones, that were airbursts (took place in the atmosphere), and so destroyed the atmosphere of Mars and changed many of its surface features. As further evidence for his claim, he also says:

"Vitrified soil, etched with acid, has been found at the sites of both hypothetical explosions, but nowhere else on Mars. This mineral resembles 'trinitite,' the melt glass found at the site of nuclear explosions. So I consider my hypothesis is being supported by new data."

Trinitite is the "vitrified" glass that is a byproduct of nuclear explosions, where rock, stone, and even pottery or bricks turn into a form of glass. It takes immense heat to do this, from either volcanism, an asteroid impact, or nuclear blasts. By the way, vitrified pottery, bones, and bricks were found at the ancient sites of Mohenjo-Daro and Harappa in India, both of which are suspected of having been struck by nuclear blasts, as well.

Chapter Conclusion: Was there a war on Mars? Tantalizing clues, even some hard evidence seems to indicate this could have been a real possibility. Geological evidence, including the Valles Marineris, could be remnants of such a catastrophe and might well be. Isotopes on Mars also point to some sort of nuclear cataclysm, whether natural or intelligently caused. Vitrified glass could also be the consequence of such nuclear blasts. Moreover, since too much time would have erased this evidence, it couldn't have happened all that long ago.

Nevertheless, what was the exact nature of such a war if it did take place? Do we have data to tell us this? Is there really enough evidence even to think this war might have actually occurred? In the next chapters, we will discuss all this in more depth.

PART IV—A MARTIAN WAR?

CHAPTER 9—What Kind Of Martian War?

Ancient texts speak of the gods' lightning bolts. Now, we already have some idea of what might have taken place on Mars in the form of a war, but there are, of course, a number of possible scenarios and variations of these that could have played out. The scenarios would be different, based on just whom the participants were, and why the war happened.

Given all this, can we know anything more about something that took place so long ago, perhaps as much as half a billion years, but probably much more recently according to Dr. Brandenburg? Do we have any other sources of possible evidence? By this, I mean besides what look like potential ruins on Mars, those radioactive elements found there, a strangely massive canyon, vitrified stone, and that "dichotomy" of Mars where the southern half is over five kilometers higher in altitude (generally) than the northern half? Well, we just might be able to find some contributing evidence to this idea from right here on Earth.

Early legends of humanity? Again, all around the world, ancient cultures had their myths and legends that date from even much earlier times than those civilizations themselves. They were handed down, first by word of mouth to each successive generation, and then finally, in the form of written material. Whether the Norse god, Thor's powerful hammer that discharged great energy, Odin's ability to hurl lightning bolts, the Greek/Roman god, Zeus/Jupiter's ability to do the same, and so many other legends of gods hurling great energy, early humans may have actually witnessed such events for real themselves.

Although, perhaps this was not in the form of actual gods doing this, but rather something else, such as spaceships or whatever, attacking their opponents. As seen from Earth and looking up at our skies, such an interplanetary war would have been awe-inspiring and surely would have left racial memories—what we now think of as legends and myths.

Remember, early humanity often thought of the planets as gods, more often than not, and this is the reason the planets are named for them now. So, if, say, a god (planet?) hurled or received a "thunderbolt" (plasma burst, or nuclear holocaust) of immense power, then this would account for why we now attribute such powers to that god, because humans witnessed something on this colossal scale. Such an event would have left an indelible mark on early civilizations, or racial memories by those who might have originally witnessed such an event transpire in the heavens. The "gods" were at war, no less. Oddly, Mars itself is the subject of one such ancient legend...

Still, one has to wonder how a planet could hurl what amounts to a plasma bolt of power. This, on the face of it, would seem impossible. However, such a thing could be conceivable if one believes in the following theory, one we touched on briefly already:

Electric Theory Of The Universe. Again, the Electric Theory of the Universe, which says that electricity, and therefore the often streams of plasma created with electricity, had a much stronger influence on the creation of galaxies and solar systems than we currently think. Once more, the theory hypothesizes that in our early solar system, with the massive number of protoplanets, dust rings/clouds, asteroids, meteors, etc., that it would have been easy for the powerful radiation of our young sun to "energize" those objects, that is charge them so they carried positive or negative electric charges.

This isn't nearly as weird an idea as it might seem. We do know that Earth already does this with its magnetic field, interactions with cosmic rays, interaction with solar radiation...all these combine to produce electrical effects. The auroras at the north and south poles show this. Thunderstorms demonstrate there is a difference in electrical charges at times between our atmosphere and the ground. Erupting volcanoes, too, can cause lightning to discharge in the cloud of gas, smoke, and ejecta they release. Electricity, it does seem, shows its effects throughout nature.

Moreover, this sort of thing isn't limited to Earth. Mighty Jupiter actually even produces its own radio waves, gives off radiation, and more. Planets, Jupiter included, have auroras in their polar regions, as well. Therefore, there is no doubt the planets do generate electromagnetic fields, and these fields can be intense! For instance, try to orbit Jupiter too closely without a great deal of protection and you will die of the radiation the planet emanates in its radiation belts.

If you think some of this radiation isn't intense or powerful, think again! For instance, the magnetosphere of Jupiter is by far and away the most powerful of all the planets in the solar system. The magnetic field produced is 18,000 times more powerful than the one that we have surrounding our Earth!

Therefore, the hypothesis that in the earlier solar system, and for a long time after its formation, there were excessive electric charges that would build up in the dust rings that still enveloped our solar system along with the new planets cannot be dismissed out of hand. Discharges of incredible power and ferocity according to the Electric Universe Theory, might have gone on then, and for a long time afterward. Moreover, when protoplanets collided, there could be an unbelievable discharge of current arcing between them (using space dust, gas, or whatever as the medium to do this?).

As mentioned earlier, later, as the solar system "settled down," as one researcher of the theory put it, and the dust rings finally had been consumed by the protoplanets and/or begun to just disperse due to planetary gravitation of the various planets orbiting the sun, this sort of arcing would have reduced. The arcing or discharges of raw power would eventually have just about ceased altogether, but on rare occasion, they still might have occurred. At least, this is the theory.

Actually, despite the compelling nature of aspects of it, we have little hard evidence for such natural discharges, again, never having witnessed anything of the sort. Therefore, this is still only a theory, and one with little actual hard evidence (in the form of witnesses such events) to support it. However, if such plasma arcing once did exist, could some early invaders of Mars and our solar system have somehow utilized these massive charge buildups to power their plasma weapons?

Again, this is just a theory, and frankly, I find the idea of an alien race being able to do such a thing a bit unlikely. Although perhaps possible, I don't find such a thing very probable. Therefore, as an idea of how Mars was destroyed by aliens harnessing such powers as planetary electrical charges just doesn't appeal to me. Yet, I can't say for sure if this did not happen.

Human Made Plasma Weapons. Nor is the idea of massive discharges of electricity and the creation of plasma along with them limited to just the Electric Universe Theory. Humans have been attempting with some considerable success of late in accomplishing the same results, although not on such massive planetary scales...not yet, at least, or so we hope. Any sort of "death ray," "ray gun," etc., is principally based on the idea of discharging a "ray" or "bolt" of superheated plasma, and our efforts to accomplish this are moving right along. Wikipedia lists a number of such attempts currently going on right now to achieve this goal, or to create things very much like a plasma weapon. Wikipedia lists:

"The MARAUDER (Magnetically Accelerated Ring to Achieve Ultra-high Directed-Energy and Radiation) project.

Plasma torches, which have existed for some years, project plasma streams a foot at most, and are used to cut metal and concrete.

The plasma gun as used in plasma physics.

Shiva Star is an attempt to make a real plasma-firing directed-energy weapon for use in space.

Microscopic, very short plasma bursts from Nd:YAG lasers are used in medicine, most widely in ophthalmology.

There are several Tesla Coil-based devices (DIY Plasma Gun and Arc Attack) that produce electrical plasma streams but only for entertainment and general interest.

The Electrolaser.

A makeshift plasma railgun has been constructed using 3D printing."

This means that we are well underway to achieving such weapons ourselves. In addition, the more power we supply them, the more powerful such weapons will become in the future.

Furthermore, this is not a new idea. In President Reagan's "Star Wars" program (Strategic Defense Initiative), started in 1983, envisioned exploding hydrogen bombs in space. A waiting satellite would receive some of this exploding energy and would use it to fire a single powerful x-ray beam, or particle beam at a target in space, or down on Earth. The satellite, of course, would be ultimately consumed in the original nuclear blast, but not before having achieved its purpose of firing off a very powerful beam. The size and power of a plasma weapon is only limited by its energy supply, and even now, those energy sources can be very powerful, indeed!

What this means is that an ancient war on or around Mars could well have used similar devices, perhaps much more powerful ones. In addition, they could have been incredibly destructive.

Another type of weapon that could be used is a "mass accelerator." This simply means that one takes a mass (bullet, cannonball, rock, asteroid, or whatever) and then one accelerates it to a very high speed. Think of something like a slingshot, but only much more high tech. We do that with missiles now in a sense. By using the thrust of the rocket carrying them, we accelerate the nuclear warheads (the mass). They go much faster than a bullet does, for instance. However, they do not use such kinetic energy to increase their explosive yield. Still, we could use the same thing, or something else (anything that would fling a mass at incredibly high speeds) to accomplish this goal.

The idea here is that one could just as easily use objects in space this same way. A small asteroid impact on Earth is far more devastating because of the high speed at which that little asteroid is traveling, much higher a speed than even a nuclear missile. All the kinetic energy that asteroid has in flying at high velocity through space has to be released upon impact and that energy translates into devastation. One could see how a Martian war with an alien race might involve such drastic measures, especially when one considers how close Mars is to the Asteroid Belt—a ready supply of mass to use as weapons against the planet.

Was someone using mass acceleration and/or plasma weapons at some time in the past? Was there an interplanetary or even interstellar war in which Mars did not fare at all well? Intriguing questions and some have come up with equally intriguing answers.

For example, Joseph Farrell, a physicist, has written a book in which he claims there was just such a war. He asserts there is evidence throughout our solar system of massively catastrophic occurrences. He even claims (and he's hardly the first in this), that the Asteroid Belt constitutes the remains of a planet destroyed in such an attack. Others also claim that Mars might just be what is left of that destroyed planet, Phaeton.

Farrell cites the fact that many or our solar system's planets bare marked signs of having undergone calamitous events. He points out, for instance Uranus. The planet has actually flipped over and is revolving on its "side" because of a calamitous event. He further states that other planets have ended up with bizarre tilts to their axis because of such a war, as well.

Others have theorized similar things. Immanuel Velikovsky hypothesized the solar system, about 10,000 years ago, had many of the planets' orbits and axis of tilt perturbed by the arrival of Venus, which he felt either had a much different orbit once, or was a rogue world captured by our sun. As it moved into our solar system, the orbits and axis tilts of other worlds were perturbed.

Similarly, David Talbott, a scholar of comparative mythology believed something similar has occurred in our solar system. After combing and sifting through an incredible amount of myths and legends, he felt he had discovered clues and/or evidence from such sources that not only Mars, but Saturn, too, occupied different orbits, both being much closer to Earth at one time. Visually, he concluded, they would have appeared quite near each other in our night sky.

Moreover, even as Velikovsky claimed, Talbott also stated that this early configuration of the two planets, being closer together and closer to Earth would have caused geological upheavals on our planet when Venus (again, about 10,000 or so years ago, and even as Velikovsky also claimed) entered the solar system and perturbed the orbits of those two planets. What would those geological upheavals be? Well, among other things, there would have been earthquakes and resulting tsunamis, volcanoes, and floods. Some of these would be on a truly enormous scale.

Talbott further goes on to say that after an initial period of this instability, the solar system would have settled down with various planets having had the tilt of their axis changed, and even their orbits altered. This would be, as he described it, a sort of "Golden Age" of stability.

However, this would slowly have altered over time until once again the situation became drastic. Planets, slowly drifting into new orbits and configurations would have caused this increasing instability.

The result? As the planets neared each other, not only were their orbits further perturbed, but there would have been electromagnetic discharges between certain planets. In other words, extraordinarily huge lightning or plasma bolts would have struck those worlds involved. Talbott further claims that the canyon, Valles Marineris, on Mars was the result of such an exceptionally huge plasma discharge.

Talbott goes further. He also claims that early humanity witnessed some of these events. Furthermore, they recorded these happenings the only way they could at the time, as pictographs and drawings in the form of rock paintings. Moreover, early legends of the gods and their weapons, gods at war with each other, and even the death of the gods, as with the Norse legend of Gotterdammerung (the dusk or "twilight of the gods"), all are attempts to describe what was witnessed in heaven and the consequential catastrophes that then engulfed the Earth.

To reinforce this theory, Talbott stresses the universality of the concept of the cosmic wheel in mythology, as well as the idea of gods hurling thunderbolts. Those thunderbolts were actually plasma bolts that struck Mars, for example.

If the idea of Mars and other planets occupying different orbits were correct, then humanity would have had a ringside seat at the time at these cosmic events. Such events, indeed, would have left a mark on the human historical psyche. Since most of this would have happened well before writing was developed, the tales of the events would have been handed down until the fact of their authenticity became obscured to the point where now we just view them as myths and legends, or so Talbott argues.

Talbott's work is a synthesis of his own research, but also that of Wal Thornhill, who theorized the electrical nature of the universe as being far more than scientists had previously considered. Mind you, if all this sounds too bizarre to be at all believable, then one should remember that Talbott had acquired by anyone's standards over the years an impressive archive of myths and legends. These were all carefully searched for similar threads of information. These, he found repeatedly. There were recurring themes of gods, thunderbolts, and catastrophic events and this was worldwide! He has correlated a direct link between just about every ancient symbol and mention of such things, and as one researcher put it, found "a direct correspondence."

Chapter Conclusion: The question in the title of this chapter, What Kind of War, has now been at least partially answered if we are to believe even some of what these researchers claim. If there was such a war, it left its mark on the entire solar system, it seems, and in a very big way. The consequences, as Talbott and others contend, left our solar system and its planets with new orbits far different from the old ones. Mars, for instance, has that highly elliptical orbit that Earth does not. Additionally, most cosmologists now claim that our planets did migrate to different orbits about the solar system and the orbits they have now are not the orbits they once started out with.

Whether this happened long ago, or just 10,000 years or so ago, is the point of argument, not the idea of planets changing their orbits. After all, the word, planet, comes from the Greek and means, literally, "wanderer."

Furthermore, the catastrophic events of those days caused planets to shift their axial tilts, sometimes drastically, as with Uranus. Planets were left scarred by the catastrophic nature of that war, as well. Therefore, we have an idea of the kind of war that might have taken place, what it caused, and the damage it may have done to our solar system. Now, let's look at who might have been doing the fighting.

CHAPTER 10—Who Fought The War?

The provocative question in all this is just who fought the war? And therein lies the problem. If a war was fought, then conspiracy theorists are in no short supply as to who was involved. In fact, we have almost too many choices to consider. Here are just some examples of what they theorize, but these are by no means all, just the major ones:

1. Native Martians fought aliens from "elsewhere."

2. Native Martians fought native Martians.

3. Humans once had an advanced civilization on Earth and fought the Martians in a devastating war where both sides lost much. The Martians lost a livable home world, civilization, and their lives, and we became a retrograde culture, one where all our prior greatness and most of its attainments became lost and completely forgotten. We suffered "racial amnesia."

4. We were the Martians and aliens attacked us. We lost our home world and migrated to Earth, again becoming a retrograde culture that had to struggle back up the technological slope to where we are today, but with our racial memories erased by time, again, racial amnesia. We will discuss this in more death in a later chapter.

5. An interstellar civilization (some claim the Sumerian Anunnaki might have been this) had outposts in our solar system, Mars and largely, Earth, being among them. An interstellar war broke out among the races and our solar system was an area where a great battle was fought. After the war, the aliens either withdrew entirely, left our system, or went into hiding.

There are more, but these should suffice to give one the idea of just how many and how varied these conspiracy theories are. All of them are intriguing possibilities, but not all of them can be correct...if any are.

Now the question also arises, is there any truth to any of them? Well if there was a war involving Mars, and there is some tantalizing evidence to suggest there just might have been, as we've seen with Dr. Brandenburg's theory, then which theory best fits the facts we now have with regard to the idea of such a war possibly having occurred?

Well, let's summarize those facts briefly here:

1. Fact: Again, Mars is an exhausted planet, with little atmosphere left. The world is a dry place with some water still, but nothing like it once had. The planet is cold. Moreover, Mars has also lost its magnetosphere, which we know it had at one time, that electromagnetic shield such as Earth still has, and which protected the Martian atmosphere for dispersing into space, which it has since been doing.

2. Fact: Given all the available evidence, Mars was once a much warmer and wetter place. Now, this is no more.

3. Fact: There is evidence Mars suffered some kind of great catastrophe. Many scientists currently find there is considerable evidence to support the idea of some large impact, and this does seem to be the case.

4. Fact: Mars has an odd orbit, highly elliptical. Moreover, the orbit of Mars is not quite in the plane of the other planets in the solar system.

5. Fact: Mars has two moons, Deimos, which is slowly orbiting further away from Mars, and Phobos, an odd moon. Phobos has strange grooves running all over its surface. It also has a huge crater, Stickney crater, and a "monolith."

6. Fact: Phobos has a strange orbit; again, one that will see the moon destroyed in the not too distant future, on a geological timescale.

7. Fact: Phobos has a low density, too low for its size. Therefore, some mainstream scientists conjecture it may really be a loose pile of rubble with a thin crust holding it together.

8. Fact: There are numerous "anomalous" items found on the surface of Mars. Some are vague and require a very active imagination to see something "real" in them, such as some of the so-called statues, skulls, bones, etc., while others seem quite convincing as real oddities, such as the "domes" and the "tracks." The number of these oddities keeps growing as we spot more of them. Again, although many can be put down to the human mind playing tricks on itself and seeing things that aren't really there, as with the phenomenon mentioned earlier in this book, pareidolia, but others do actually seem to be something odd or strange, and look out of place on the Martian surface.

9. Fact: There is the mystery of that gigantic "Grand Canyon of Mars," the Valles Marineris, which stretches across the planet almost as far as the United States is wide, and on average much deeper than our Grand Canyon here on Earth. How was it created?

10. Fact: Mars does have some radioactive trace elements on its surface and in its atmosphere. Scientists (some) conjecture it might have been the result of a natural "georeactor" (a naturally occurring situation that results in an atomic explosion of immense proportions), while others question this. Some of the isotopes are definitely of the type left over from a nuclear blast, so there does seem to have been at least some type of such an explosion, either through the natural means mentioned, or created by some intelligence. Nobody knows.

11. Fact: Thermal scanning of the planet's surface show a grid-like pattern below the surface, and it covers close to 300 square miles in area! Again, since thermal imaging means that only things giving off heat will show up in the photographs, this region must be giving off heat.

Where is this heat coming from? What would energize a grid pattern so huge, and below the surface to the point where an orbiting and rather primitive (by our standards today) satellite thermal imaging camera could pick up the image?

The answer, of course, is it has to be either volcanic or radioactive in nature to give off heat. Since there is no sign of any volcanism in this region, or any having been there, then one can reasonably conclude it must be a radioactive region.

Furthermore, on Earth, we have no such radioactive areas that are in grid-like patterns that form naturally. We do have the ancient ruins of two cities in India, Mohenjo-Daro (very grid-like), and Harappa. Of course, these are not natural, but manmade.

In addition, many researchers think these must have been nuked at one time, since again, there is no naturally occurring radiation of such extremes in the surrounding regions, only in and very close to the cities themselves.

So given all this, was a city on Mars "nuked?" Then, were the ruins of that great Martian metropolis slowly buried by the dust storms that plague Mars over the millennia? It could well be that is exactly what happened. Otherwise, how do we account for a grid-like pattern below the surface of Mars and one that is also "warm," as well, warm enough to show up on a satellite orbiting the planet, even when covered by surface material, soil, debris, and such?

How do we use all this information, all these facts to come to any conclusions about the nature of the war? Well, if there was one (and I tend to think there might have been), we can at least settle on the results. That is, Mars was killed. Again, the planet lost much of its atmosphere, had its surface devastated and changed in massive ways, lost its magnetosphere, and had a great gouge ripped across its surface, the Valles Marineris Canyon. A once warmer and wet world literally died. Again, there are signs of nuclear detonations having taken place of the "airburst" variety.

Now, sorry for having had to repeat some of that information, but we are going to use it here as a tool to try to figure out which of the above main scenarios mentioned, best fit these results of such a possible war. Well, the problem is that all of them do to some degree, but perhaps some do more than others do. We need to know even more. To gain more insight into the answers, we have to look for another way to try to resolve the issue of who was involved and what happened. We need some other source of information, as well, to add to the facts above. Luckily, I think we have that.

Our own ancient human texts of various civilizations, as mentioned, perhaps can give us some more insight into all of this:

1. Vedic Texts. As mentioned earlier, the Vedic texts of the Hindus in India, especially the Mahabharata and the Ramayana talk of an ancient great war that occurred long before even those ancient texts were written. The texts speak of gods, such as Krishna, who ruled over humans, and there is also evidence of an early empire in India and Pakistan called the Rama Empire. Not much is known about this empire or civilization, but here is a summary of what is thought to be the case:

The Rama Empire, regarded by many researchers, but certainly not all, was originally thought to have been a mythical civilization that started around 8,000 years ago in the Indus Valley region of the Indian Subcontinent. Centered largely in eastern Pakistan, it also occupied part of the western area of present-day India.

According to the Vedic Texts, the Rama Empire was destroyed in a great war that took place on Earth, in space, and even on the Moon. Flying vehicles, called vimanas, of varying sizes and power supposedly fought in that war, some with human pilots, considered the most trusted servants of the "gods" (read: aliens, here).

Powerful weapons supposedly were used, as described in the Mahabharata in high detail. According to one source, the texts state:

"Gurkha, flying a swift and powerful vimana hurled a single projectile charged with the power of the Universe. An incandescent column of smoke and flame, as bright as ten thousand suns, rose with its entire splendor…"

And:

"It was a
n unknown weapon, an iron thunderbolt, a gigantic messenger of death, which reduced to ashes the entire races of the Vrishnis and the Andhakas. The corpses were so burned as to be unrecognizable. Hair and nails fell out; pottery broke without apparent cause and the birds turned white. After a few hours all foodstuffs were infected...to escape from this fire the soldiers threw themselves in streams to wash themselves and their equipment."

And this, as well:

"Dense arrows of flame, like a great shower, issued forth upon creation, encompassing the enemy. A thick gloom swiftly settled upon the Pandava hosts **[Nuclear**

winter?]. *All points of the compass were lost in darkness. Fierce wind began to blow upward, showering dust and gravel. Birds croaked madly... the very elements seemed disturbed. The earth shook, scorched by the terrible violent heat of this weapon. Elephants burst into flame and ran to and fro in frenzy."*

Obviously, and as others have stated, this is a very close description of a nuclear strike, complete with flash and flash heat, major devastation, shock wave, radiation poisoning, and fallout. For a myth to describe so closely something we've only invented in the last century as a weapon is amazing, because the accuracy of the description in so many details is so spot on!

Is there evidence to support the Vedic Texts with regard to there once having been a nuclear conflagration on Earth? Actually, there is some astonishing confirmation to support this idea and precisely where one would think to find it...where the Vedic Texts were written. For instance:

Mohenjo-Daro and Harappa: Mohenjo-Daro, a buried ancient city in Pakistan has unearthed some extreme oddities. In this grim, grid-like, laid out city (ruins) skeletons were discovered. Many of these just lay where they fell in the streets or elsewhere, some actually clasping hands, as if they were struck down in flight, or simply did this as they faced their imminent deaths.

This, however, is not the only bizarre thing found. Several of the skeletons were radioactive, and as one report said, five times the background radiation of the region! In fact, some researchers insist the radioactive levels of some of the skeletons registered about the same as skeletons found in the aftermath of the nuclear attacks on Nagasaki and Hiroshima in Japan at the end of World War II.

However, in my research, I couldn't find evidence for this higher level of radiation, where it was the same as at Hiroshima or Nagasaki, so whether that extreme level is true or not, is hard to say. Again, many skeletons in India were just lying in the streets, some of them holding hands, as if some great doom had suddenly overtaken them in their flight. A skeleton found in the ruins of another ancient city showed radiation levels 50 times greater than normal!

Moreover, a circular area, reminiscent of a crater was also discovered at Mohenjo-Daro and this had the outer edges surrounded by vitrified stone and/or bricks, something that normally only happens in nuclear explosions near ground zero, or from volcanic activity or an asteroid impact.

Nor is Mohenjo-Daro alone in this respect, because vitrified stones have been found in some of the ruins of ancient fortresses in Scotland, Germany, Ireland, India, and other places. In short, something big happened a long time ago and it seems to have involved nukes! Moreover, it seems it just might have been worldwide.

Nor does the evidence of a nuclear attack stop there. Pottery pieces were also discovered in the remains of the city's ruins, and these, too, were often vitrified. No asteroid impact occurred in this region in human historic times that we know of or even before. No volcanic activity took place in this area, either, so that only leaves the possibility of nuclear attacks on these sites.

The odd thing about Mohenjo-Daro, and its sister city, Harappa, is both these cities show signs of being the targets of nuclear strikes, and yet, they don't seem to date back to the supposed time of the Rama Empire and its demise, but rather came much later, around 1800 to as early as 2600 BCE. Was there more than one attack? Did the Rama Empire die during a nuclear war? Did subsequent cities in the same region again suffer the same fate centuries later? It would appear so...

A few more oddities about Mohenjo-Daro, as a National Geographic article referred to it (see references for link):

"Faceless" Indus Valley City Puzzles Archae-ologists."

The reason the article calls the city "faceless" is that we still have no idea who lived there, who the inhabitants were. In addition, the city lacks any unique identifying aspects. As mentioned, the city was designed with what seems a very high knowledge of engineering for the times, too high, perhaps... The city had plumbing, incredible drainage systems designed to wash streets and allow the water to drain cleanly away.

The once thriving city of Mohenjo-Daro
Photo credit: AnnoyzView, Public Domain

Mohenjo-Daro ruins
Source: Public Domain

There were no palaces or grand city structures, as almost every city on Earth, old and new, seems to boast. Instead, the type of dwellings were almost monotonous in cubist-style construction. In fact, the city seems to have been either classless in its social makeup or the metropolis was designed for a single class, probably laborers. If so, for whom was this city of laborers laboring?

There were also plenty of shops and stores for the citizens to frequent, as well. Yet, we don't know their language, can't decipher it. Again, the cities not only lacked palaces, but also temples, which again, is very strange! What city today does not have churches and/or temples? What other ancient city completely lacked such structures?

Even Egyptians crowded their metropolises with such buildings, as did the Greeks, Rome, and everyone else. Nor do many of the other civilizations show the degree of design, planning, and sophistication of these two ancient cities.

As with Harappa (which dates back to the same period, or perhaps just a bit further, 3000 BCE, Mohenjo-Daro also showed refined and educated tastes in tool designs, jewelry, pottery, and much else. Again, there were no palaces found, no grand edifices of any real sort, although the cities had walls around them and were well planned and executed in design.

Lonar Crater: This crater dates at being just under 50,000 years old by some experts. However, the crater's formation is an enigma. No meteoric material of any sort has ever been found anywhere in, on, or around the crater, not so much as a trace, so it is apparently not the result of an impact, presumably. The crater is the only known one made in solid basalt and this is important, because basalt is a very dense and hard rock. Whatever punched a hole in it had to have been very powerful, indeed.

Moreover, the crater does not seem to be the result of volcanic activity. Yet, something massive and catastrophic occurred there some time long ago. Glass spherules, the result of intense heat abound near the site. Moreover, the area was "shocked" by a powerful blast because evidence for this exists in the form of "shocked quartz." Therefore, some scientists still theorize the crater must be meteoric in origin based on this fact alone, since such impacts do produce shocked quartz. However, so do nuclear explosions.

Again, since no meteorite remains of any sort have been found at all, either of those causes, meteorite or nuclear, is still anyone's guess. However, since the crater formed in basalt, a dense and very hard rock, one would have expected such a powerful impact would also have wreaked damage on the area surrounding the crater, as well, such as flinging large boulders of basalt and more about the landscape. This does not seem to be the case. There are no signs of any ejecta on this level in the area, and basalt takes a VERY long time to erode away. Therefore, we should see some sign of such basalt ejecta still. We don't.

So is this more evidence for a nuclear explosion having occurred so long ago, and then again occurring around 3000 to 4,000 years ago, something nuclear in nature, but also something occurring closer to 50,000 years ago! Again, two nuclear wars?

Radioactive Ash, Rajasthan, India. A layer of radioactive ash was found after people in the area constantly suffered from cancers, illnesses, and even birth defects at a much higher rate than normal. This was in Rajasthan, India. When investigators began checking for causes for such health issues, they discovered there was a lay of ash in the soil in the immediate region and that it was radioactive. With no other recourse, the Indian government quarantined the site. What could account for this highly radioactive area is a mystery, unless, of course, the place suffered the same sort of attack that Mohenjo-Daro would seem to have.

Chapter Conclusion: We've covered a lot of information in this chapter. We have learned Mars might very well have been the victim of some type of a great war, as Earth might have been, as well. Radioactive sites in India and Pakistan show some sort of nuclear devices might have been used. Judging by the vitrification, the higher radiation levels at some sites and the strange nature (no palaces or temples) of those two ancient cities, Harappa and Mohenjo-Daro, points to something strange having happened there, and a very different sort of people or society having lived there.

First, the cities themselves were more designed as livable fortresses than cities, and yet they were cities. Their level of technical sophistication was high, their design, and layout admirable. Yet, none of this saved them. Moreover, archaeologists can't understand how a people who lived practically even before the dawn of recorded history could have such technical capabilities. Where did they get them? Who were they? We can't even understand their written language or its origins!

Both these sites and others in India and Pakistan, as well as around the world, show evidence of vitrification of not only bricks and stones, but even vitrified pottery. Therefore, we have to assume some type of nuclear holocaust in fact, did occur. It seems it may have occurred more than once. The Lonar Crater would seem to indicate devastation took place around 50,000 years ago. Yet the evidence from Harappa and Mohenjo-Daro, shows something "else" also happened much later on, closer to our own time, and only around 5,000 years ago.

Based on this, we can assume that two "somethings" took place, both nuclear in nature and widely spaced in time. Both of these events were on Earth.

However, the Vedic texts speak of a great war in space, on the Moon (and on Earth) with many alien races involved. The Sumerian cuneiform writings speak of the Anunnaki, beings who came from the sky and ruled over humanity, even created humanity to be their slave laborers (hence, the creation of cities like Mohenjo-Daro and Harappa, with their odd designs?). Then, something calamitous happened to them, as well, and the texts speak of war and ultimately human rebellion during that war. Nor, according to the texts, was this war on a small scale, but took place around the solar system, and apparently elsewhere, as well. An interstellar war?

Hard Evidence: Well, there are the radioactive skeletons and such, as mentioned. There are the vitrified bricks, stones, and pottery pieces. There are craters, but no sign of meteor impacts or volcanic activity having occurred on those sites to create them. There is radiation at some of those sites, as well.

Moreover, nobody knows who inhabited Mohenjo-Daro and Harappa. We don't understand the language they used, or their writing. We have no idea who these people were, other than they might have been the inheritors of the once mighty Rama Empire, said to have been destroyed in that great interstellar war. Furthermore, what we do know is the Indian government closed the Mohenjo-Daro site because of the dangerous levels of radioactivity discovered there! So something nuclear happened, certainly.

As for the people of that city, all we know for certain, again, is they were very good at design, layout, and execution of cities that were built more like fortresses rather than simple organically evolving metropolises. That is about it.

Why? What did these advanced people fear when no other civilization around them at the time seemed to have such technical capabilities? Where were their civic leaders, their princes, or priests? Where were there rulers and the wealthy? Why were there no palaces, temples, or other such edifices as one finds everywhere else in cities ancient and new, in not only India now, but also everywhere? Again, we simply don't know.

What we do know is that the complete absence of these at the sites is evidence in itself. It tells us what the cities were "not" like. They were not like any cities of other civilizations that we know of in those respects. They were…different, profoundly so.

However, we also have historical written records and even some hard evidence that something big, something "nuclear" took place on Earth a long time ago, perhaps twice, and it wasn't just restricted to one region, but was planet wide and apparently beyond. So if we humans didn't have a thermonuclear war back then, then just who did? Who left radioactive bomb craters and radiated people? Who detonated something that vitrified clay pottery into glass, along with bricks and even stones?

The answer to that would seem simple: if we didn't do all this, then it had to be "them." By them, of course, I mean extraterrestrials. Furthermore, whatever happened to Earth seems to have happened to Mars and even perhaps other planets or moons, as well. It might even be that the Asteroid Belt was once a planet but was destroyed. We simply don't know.

What we can only conclude based on physical evidence and historical records and the facts listed above is that an alien race, or races, perhaps including the original inhabitants of Mars, were somehow involved in a catastrophic war that badly damaged at least two planets and possibly more...

Yet, this is just one form of a possible cataclysm, an interplanetary or interstellar war. There are other types of possible cataclysms, as well.

PART V—CATACLYSMIC MARS?

CHAPTER 11—Did Mars Once Have A Different Orbit?

Now, we have just discussed the idea of a major war on Mars and perhaps on Earth, which in itself would have been a cataclysm of major proportions. Therefore, some would argue that topic should be in this section of the book, under Cataclysmic Mars. Yet, that form of catastrophe would have been the result of intelligent beings acting in a perhaps not too intelligent manner. This is why I kept it separate from this section.

Now, we have to consider there are other factors that might have caused such a cataclysm for Mars and these probably were not the direct result of a nuclear war at all, or perhaps even intelligent beings behaving badly.

You see, there is some evidence that Mars may not have always occupied its present orbit. If so, the change in that orbit could have resulted in a cataclysm for a warm and wet Mars, one that may not only have supported life, but even intelligent life. Yet, how could the orbit of Mars change so drastically as to cause such a thing?

Well, again, Mars in many respects is very earthlike. It has mountains, canyons, plains, and deserts. The planet has basin areas. There is even a region that appears to have been home to a vast if somewhat shallow sea. We also see signs of old riverbeds, lakebeds, and more. So yes, Mars was very earthlike in its physical makeup at one time. Moreover, the thicker atmosphere, the wetter planet it once was, even adds to this earthlike scenario. Does this mean Mars might have once been closer to the sun, and therefore, closer to Earth, as well?

This might just have been the case. If so, it might not only have been Earth that could have been colonized by an alien race. Some race, such as the Anunnaki (more on that later), could also have colonized Mars, as well.

What evidence do we have for this? Well, remember, we do know that Mars has a very eccentric (elliptical/oval-shaped) orbit compared to most other planets. We also know that it orbits our sun in a slightly different plane than most of the other planets, including our Earth. Something must have happened at some point in the lifespan of the red planet to cause these odd changes. Otherwise, Mars wouldn't have such an eccentric orbit or odd tilt to the plane of the solar system. In other words, "something" had to have caused this great change in its orbit. Just what was it? What provoked such an alteration in the orbit of Mars?

Moreover, also remember those carbonates we talked about in Chapter 1? They only form, as they do well enough here on Earth, if there is plenty of carbon dioxide in the atmosphere. Scientists theorized that the lack of them on Mars means that the planet must have once been closer to the sun, and then for some reason moved farther away.

Mainstream scientists theorize that Jupiter might have once been closer to our sun, as well. It seems that the giant planet, at one point, was slowly shifting its orbit inward in the solar system. Then, due to the influence of another planet (they hypothesize Saturn), its orbit was altered and it began moving outward again. Did Jupiter, with its tremendous gravitational pull, drag its neighbor, little Mars along with it?

If this occurred, then a planet that was once warm and wet would have slowly been pulled away from its place by the warm fire that is our sun. As it drifted into an outer orbit, it would grow colder, drier, and more inhospitable to life. Any advanced life on Mars would have struggled with diminishing resources, with even adequate supplies of water ultimately becoming scarce, and the surface of the planet then finally becoming inhabitable.

On Earth, wars over resources have been common throughout history. They continue even now. Imagine what it would have been like on Mars, where every year the winter grew colder, harsher, and longer, and the summers less warm, where every day meant an increasing hardship to survive. With stockpiles depleted, starvation would have set in. A great die-off would have occurred on the red planet. War, including nuclear war, might have been the final consequence of such a scenario, as mentioned in Part V of this book, as the remnants of a once advanced race fought among themselves to gain control of what little was left.

As unlikely as this scenario might seem, there is some evidence to suggest this is just what might have happened to the planet, at least as far as the planet moving. For instance, although Mars once had a thicker atmosphere, one much richer with greenhouse gases to help keep it warm, the planet, according to many scientists, was just too far from the sun in its present orbit, especially a younger sun that wasn't as bright as it is now, or throwing off as much heat, therefore.

This is normal in the evolution of our type of star, for the sun to grow brighter and slowly expand over time. Yet, this means that for Mars, in its present orbit, it simply would not have received enough light or warmth, and this despite a thicker atmosphere with more greenhouse gases. In other words, it should have still been a very cold world despite this.

So how did Mars get enough light to be such a warmer and wetter world? Even our planet, in its present orbit much closer to the sun has experienced a long series of freezing ice ages. Wouldn't a planet, as far from the younger sun as Mars is now, have been in a permanent "snowball Earth" phase, always locked in a freezing, planet-wide glacial ice age? Theoretically, it should have been. Nonetheless, evidence shows that it did once have liquid water. Remember that shallow ocean, those lakes, and rivers Mars once had? How could this have been given this information?

Well, the answer seems to be that Mars had to have been closer to the younger sun in order to be this way— warmer and wetter. Additionally, we are fairly certain that Jupiter's orbit, too, has changed over the billions of years, and with Mars being so close to Jupiter, the planet's orbit should have been drastically affected, as well.

Chapter Conclusion: Did Mars once occupy a different orbit, perhaps one closer to the sun, and so closer to the Earth? This could well have been the case. With the red planet's eccentric orbit, the fact its orbital plane varies slightly from the solar plane, and the fact that scientists theorize it must have been warmer and wetter once, this could well have been the situation.

The death of Mars, as Jupiter snagged it (or never let it go in the first place), and dragged it outwards from an orbit closer to the sun is a real possibility. After all, we now know the early solar system was far more like a deadly pinball game of planets, protoplanets, asteroids, and comets than it was like a clockwork, well run system, as we used to think it was.

Did the orbit of Mars change? It is almost a certainty something at some point had affected it, based on the available evidence. Was that something Jupiter? That would seem likely, but it isn't a foregone conclusion. Something else might have caused Mars to suffer such a calamity, and in the next chapter, we will discuss this.

As opposed to Jupiter being the culprit in all of this, other researchers think a series of large asteroid impacts may have slowly pushed Mars farther from the sun. After all, the planet, even now, is much closer to the Asteroid Belt than Earth is and so should have been subject to more collisions. Even if it wasn't originally that close the belt, it was closer than Earth by far, and that would mean more chances of asteroids striking the planet. We also know that the early solar system did see far more bombardments of comets and asteroids, but these lessened over time, as the solar system slowly cleaned itself of the worst of this sort of thing through such constant collisions.

I find this last idea, that asteroids are the culprit, less impressive than the idea that Jupiter is responsible. Firstly, we know Jupiter exerts a tremendous pull on planets in the solar system, and even affects our Earth in some ways and to some real extent, as far from that giant as we are. It would seem logical to assume that Mars, being much closer to that once migrating gas giant, would have suffered more gravitational pull from it, since the closer an object is to another in space, the greater the gravitational influence they come under.

Even so, the idea of asteroids being the perpetrator that devastated Mars by pushing it farther away from the young sun cannot be overlooked.

CHAPTER 12—The Destruction of Planet Five?

Was there once a fifth planet in our solar system, one between Mars and Jupiter? The answer is yes, there could have been, although scientists debate this hotly, and the majority think not. Where the Asteroid Belt lies now, are numerous shards of rock—asteroids—and they are of differing types. Some are large, such as Ceres, Vesta, and Pallas—very large, almost small planets in their own right. Ceres, it is theorized from the most recent available data, even has a good deal of water locked up as ice.

Other asteroids are carbonaceous in nature, have lots of carbon and other elements locked in them. Still others are solid nickel and iron and so are very dense asteroids. Others contain silver, gold, platinum, rhodium, and other heavy metals. In short, the asteroids, combined, seem to have all the materials necessary to have once made a planet. Some scientists even theorize that the heavy nickel-iron asteroids were once the core (just like with our Earth now) of a protoplanet or protoplanets.

Yet, not all believe that the Asteroid Belt, approximately 2-1/2 times farther from the sun than the Earth, was always the Asteroid Belt. Some believe it was once a planet in its own right. Bode's Law was the first to predict that where the Asteroid Belt is now, there should have been a planet. What is Bode's Law? As Wikipedia states:

"The Titius–Bode law (sometimes termed just Bode's law) is a hypothesis that the bodies in some orbital systems, including the Sun's, orbit at semi-major axes in a function of planetary sequence. The formula suggests that, extending outward, each planet

would be approximately twice as far from the Sun as the one before. The hypothesis correctly anticipated the orbits of Ceres (in the asteroid belt) and Uranus, but failed as a predictor of Neptune's orbit and has eventually been superseded as a theory of solar system formation. It is named for Johann Daniel Titius and Johann Elert Bode."

Now, modern astronomy discredits this law, saying since it didn't correctly predict all the planets and where they should belong, it is simply wrong. Yet, Ceres is a huge asteroid, and in fact, until as recently as 2006, it was thought to be the largest asteroid. Even more to the point, it is spherical in nature, which classifies it as a dwarf planet, a newer classification for objects which are not as large as planets, but big enough for their own gravity to cause them to become spherical in shape. Moreover, the Titius-Bode Law did predict its location.

Furthermore, we have some evidence that Neptune's orbit, even as Jupiter's was, has changed. Still further, the Titius-Bode Law predicted the current orbit of the planet Uranus and it is the closest planet to Neptune. Uranus is the seventh planet from the sun and Neptune is the eighth.

Remember, there is another oddity about Uranus. Unlike any of the other planets, Uranus is "rolling along on its side," meaning that if Earth did the same, our current north and south poles would lie along the equator. Scientists theorize that something "happened" to Uranus, something big, that knocked or pulled the planet over on its "side." In fact, Uranus is the weirdo of our solar system in this regard. Its spin axis is tilted by a whopping 98 degrees, meaning it essentially spins on its side. Other planets have nowhere near such an odd angle. Jupiter has only a three-degree tilt, for example. Again, Uranus has an incredible 98-degree tilt! Something big had to have caused this one planet to be so different.

Scientists simply cannot account for the current plight of Uranus, its strange and extreme tilt. Numerous theories have been advanced, but none seems to explain the current state of affairs with the planet. The only theory that even comes close is two, or possibly even more giant collisions took place that literally knocked the planet over on its side, and changed the orbits of its moons, as well. This would require at least a minimum of two such collisions, but most scientists say it would need even more!

This presents a conundrum for astronomers and cosmologists alike. The theory of the early solar system forming from an accretion disk does not account for how such massive collisions could have occurred so early on in our solar system's history. When the planets were forming, most of the material would have been small and nowhere near the size such massive objects would be to have been able to knock Uranus out of kilter. This means that there is something wrong with our theory of how planets formed from the accretion disk.

Alternatively, it could mean that something big, or "some things" big came from somewhere else, somewhere on the edge of our early system or even from interstellar space, such as a rogue planet, perhaps one with moons. These could have passed through our solar system, affecting Neptune (gravitationally pulling it into its current orbit, which is contrary to the Titius-Bode Law prediction), toppled Uranus over on its side, and even disturbed the orbit of mighty Jupiter.

Furthermore, this "something" or "some things" might have collided with a fifth planet (now destroyed and leaving the Asteroid Belt as its remnants) and devastated it.

Remember, we know something caused Uranus to tip over. We also know that the Asteroid Belt contains all the elements for a planet in the form of asteroids. We further know that many asteroids have material only made up of what once should have been the core of a planet, because it is extremely unlikely such asteroids simply formed that way on their own. They would not have had enough gravity and/or density to have formed purely out of nickel, iron, gold, and platinum.

So was there another planet? Well, there could have been. Again, the evidence is elusive, but there is some evidence for this being true, as we've seen. At the very least, it is a reasonable hypothesis and one still considered possible by some scientists. Even so, how does this affect Mars?

The answer to that is simple; when two planets collide, and one is smashed to smithereens (or perhaps both planets), pieces fly everywhere. Mars, being the next closest world inward toward the sun from that planetary collision would have suffered impacts from the debris of such a massive catastrophe. Moreover, it does seem that Mars has suffered some type of major impact in just such a way, as well as other and lesser impacts. It has even been theorized that the moons of Mars are shards from that planet.

Therefore, the idea that Mars could have had its atmosphere ripped from it by such a collision is well within the realm of possibility, even as many scientists theorize it might have (but not necessarily from the impact of another planetary collision).

Even more to the point, our Earth, as theorized by many astronomers, also had such an impact from the planet "Theia" early on, in its existence. Was Theia a piece of that once fifth planet? It does make one wonder. We do seem to have an oversized moon as a result of the Theia impact (or so scientists say).

So Earth and Mars—were they scarred forever by such impacts? That, too, is a possibility. Did the theoretical planet "Phaeton" explode somehow and cause such shrapnel to fly throughout the solar system? We simply don't have enough data yet to decide definitively one way or the other, I'm afraid, but it is a possibility.

Chapter Conclusion: That Mars has an eccentric orbit and odd tilt to its plane of orbit around the sun is a fact. That it looks to have suffered a major impact that could have well stripped it of most of its atmosphere and "shut off" its protective magnetic field is also considered to be a high probability, rather than just a possibility.

We also have evidence of something disturbing all the planets out there, including Neptune, Uranus (causing that last to tip over on its side), and even mighty Jupiter shifting position. We also think a "mars-like" object, the planet "Theia," impacted the Earth, as well. So did something move through our solar system causing this destruction, something such as a rogue planet? Did this rogue planet disturb orbits and cause the destruction of the theorized planet Phaeton? Again, we simply don't have enough facts to know really, one way or the other, but it is an intriguing possibility.

However, we do have these oddities amongst the outer planets and those of Mars, as well. Again, "something" big happened out there. Whatever it was, the result was to leave our solar system forever changed in some enormous ways. Moreover, it might just have resulted in the death of the planet Mars and any life, intelligent or otherwise, it might have once harbored.

What we have seen here is evidence in both these last chapters dealing with a cataclysm on Mars, of some form of destruction that brought about the end of early Mars. Today, the red planet is world that appears to be slowly winding down, dying. It no longer has an active core, as Earth does. Its atmosphere is thin. Radiation pours down upon the surface, sterilizing it. Although there is still water on the planet, it is nothing compared to what scientists think was once there.

Maybe, just maybe, Mars was once like the science fiction writers of the last century thought it might be, a world that once harbored abundant life, but which then saw it all slowly die away, or alternatively, disappear overnight, in mere hours or less, from some hideous collision. Either way, one can't help but lament to some extent, the sad state of affairs that is Mars today. Whatever caused its demise as a warm and wet world, it is so no longer....

PART VI—INTELLIGENT LIFE ON MARS NOW?

CHAPTER 13—Be There Aliens There?

Now we come to the question of there being intelligent life on Mars right now, whether this is even possible. The quick answer is yes, it is possible. Then, most things are....

However, is it likely? Current scientists think not. They point out that the Martian atmosphere is very thin. The extremes of temperature on Mars, even at the equator in the Martian summertime are just that...extreme! The type of atmosphere Mars has is mostly carbon dioxide. There seems to be no vegetation at all, and even microbial life is shy in revealing itself (even if it exists at all today).

In addition, nobody has met a Martian alien. Nobody, supposedly, has spoken to one, if our scientists and researchers are to be believed. Moreover, they make a good case for the idea that nothing so complex as a sentient (intelligent) being could survive on Mars without a major effort and high technological support. This is the gist of what we are all told about the idea of Mars and intelligent Martians being alive today.

Is it true? Is Mars so dead a world when it comes to advanced life being on it? Well, we have some intriguing evidence that it just might not be as dead as scientists think. This is for a number of reasons, and I will say up front, that some of this evidence is "iffy," but some of it is rather compelling, as well. Just what information are we talking about here? Well, again, it is circumstantial but many people, some researchers included among them, point to these things:

1. High failure rate of Martian missions. As mentioned in passing earlier on in this book, the number of failed missions to Mars is huge and higher than with any other planet to which we've sent probes. Again, out of 40 missions to the planet, only 18 have managed to arrive or land there successfully. What accounts for such a high failure rate?

Well, we know that some of the missions had flaws in the calculations used to get them there, or so we are told. One even had erroneous commands sent to it. As CNN put it:

"NASA lost a $125 million Mars orbiter because a Lockheed Martin engineering team used English units of measurement while the agency's team used the more conventional metric system for a key spacecraft operation..."

Of course, that's the official excuse and it may or may not be true. It could be a cover up for something else. After all, NASA has definitely not always been very forthcoming about things that happen on its missions, or they simply remain silent and say nothing at all sometimes. Even so, if this statement is true, it was rather a basic and stupid mistake to make.

In any case, we have lost a seemingly inordinate number of very expensive missions to Mars and we aren't the only ones. For example, the Mars Observer exploded in 1993 while preparing its engines to insert the Observer into orbit. In 1999, two successive missions failed.

Other countries have faced this sort of problem, as well. For instance, Japan's first mission to Mars failed because the rocket went off course. This was in 1998. Russia had a disastrous Martian probe attempt, a number of them. In 1995, the upper stage of the rocket failed and the result was radioactive debris landing somewhere in the mountains of the Andes.

What am I implying here by all this? Well, perhaps Mars is just a very hard planet to send probes to, although why that would be is not immediately obvious. One would think Jupiter or Saturn would be the more difficult, what with them both having moons and rings systems, intense radiation belts, etc., for probes to navigate through and get by successfully. Even Venus has been far easier for us to send successful missions to than Mars has been. Is it just really bad luck, or it is "something else?"

Many conspiracy theorists, and bona fide researchers, as well, wonder if some other factor might be at work here other than just incredibly rotten luck for all of Earth's countries, whether Japan, the United States, Russia, India, or whoever. These conspiracy theorists and researchers think, of course, that "someone," or "something" most likely not human, has deliberately interfered with the success of these missions. They point, in particular to a failed Russian mission, to back them on this contention. In addition, with this particular case, we do have some photographic evidence, and a statement from the Russian authorities on what happened...

This occurred on a Russian mission named "Fobos-2" as the Russians called it, or "Phobos-2" as we do in English. This mission to Mars had a very peculiar ending. On March 1989, the Phobos-2 mission ended abruptly in disaster for the probe, and this is what began tongues wagging on the conspiracy circuit, but also among mainstream scientists, as well.

A little background: Russia, at the time being the Soviet Union, had suffered a string of bad luck when it came to their Martian missions. The first run of such missions going awry took place from 1960 to 1965 when a number of probes, small ones, all failed to make it all the way to Mars.

This might be forgiven, what with the more primitive technology of the day, but it happened again in the years 1969 through 1973 and these were larger, better-designed probes. They, too, didn't do very well. Then, in 1988, the Soviet Union tried yet again, with two separate missions/probes this time. This time, they put all their effort into the project, using the very latest in the way of computers, rockets, etc. Moreover, it carried smaller probes that were to be launched toward Phobos to land two small packets of data-gathering devices on that weird little moon.

Things did not go well. The first mission failed entirely, supposedly due to a mistaken command, as it traveled toward Mars. (Sound familiar, as with NASA's later "mistaken" set of sent commands? Perhaps an excuse that's getting used a little too much and too often?) The other mission did make it to Mars, but had problems on board on the way. By the time it arrived, the probe had little power left for its communications system, and so had to rely on the last working radio, and by no means the best one for communications.

The good news is the Soviet Union had finally managed to get something to Mars. In addition, the probe did as commanded, attaining the correct orbit for the planet. Moreover, it also managed to adjust this orbit to coincide getting closer to Phobos, which it also did.

By our standards today, the probe was still rather "clunky," in that instead of simply being able to aim its cameras at Phobos, the whole craft had to keep rotating in order for the cameras to focus on the little moon. Even so, the probe was working to the best of its capabilities in this regard. It took a number of photos of Phobos.

However, suddenly, the data flow via the weak radio ceased. This was, to some degree, expected. They knew the power supply for the radio was draining quickly. However, there were still short spurts of data, and these suggested that the probe's antenna was gyrating, so the signals were sometimes correctly aligned with Earth and other times not. This happened just before the probe failed completely.

Luckily, some photographs had been received before the probe utterly ceased to function. One of them showed what appeared to be a huge cigar-shaped shadow on the surface of Mars. Another photo caught the same sort of shape, but this one was in space, near the moon, Phobos! This was no shadow, but a long, sun-lit, object, also cigar, or cylinder shaped. Then, after getting these photos, something seemed to "attack," as some researchers put it, the Soviet probe, causing it's antenna to spin around, before knocking the probe out completely. A "one-two punch?" Russian authorities used the term "impact" in describing what caused the probe's demise. In other words, "something" hit it.

With regard to the photos: an official Soviet news outlet said:

"The features are either on the Martian surface or in the lower atmosphere. The features are between 20 and 25 kilometers wide and do not resemble any known geological formation. They are spindle - shaped and proving to be intriguing and puzzling."

The image appears to be that of a shadow, long and in the shape of a "thin ellipse." In short, it seems to be the shadow of that something floating in space near Phobos. However, it couldn't possibly have been the shadow of Phobos, itself. Shadows of Phobos have been seen, and they are rounded, uneven at the edges. This photo was not. Please see photographs below:

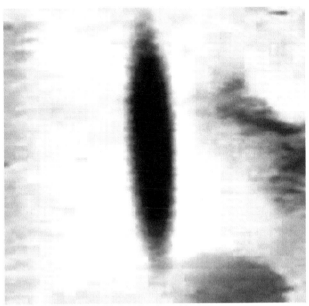

Shadow of alien spacecraft on Mars?
Source: Public Domain

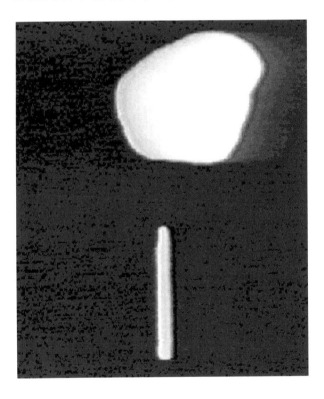

Alien spacecraft near Phobos?
Source: Public Domain

The long cylindrical thing above, far more meets the criteria for the shape of something that would cause such an odd shadow to appear on Mars. Based on the image of the "cylinder," Soviet scientists were able to calculate the dimensions of the object. They described it as nearly 20 kilometers in length and 1.5 kilometers in width. Huge! Nor was the thing some sort of illusion since the object was visible in the infrared and standard optical instruments alike aboard the Fobos-2 probe. Dr. Becklake stated the object appeared as:

"...something that is between the spacecraft and Mars, because we can see the Martian surface below it."

In addition, under some pressure by just about everyone, the Soviets released a portion of a televised image and it contained two rather strange things. These were sent by Fobos-2 just before the probe was destroyed. One of the images was of a grid of lines near a portion of the Mars equator.

These lines were not standard, with some being narrow, others being wider, and they ultimately gave the impression of rectangular shapes arranged in parallel formation over an area that it has been calculated must have covered about 600 square kilometers, roughly.

Furthermore, the infrared camera picked this image up, meaning that it seemed to be getting a picture of something generating some heat from some source and that the image was probably of something below ground.

The radioactive ruins of a Martian city? Could be... Dr. Becklake seemed to think so. Moreover, since the Soviets never released the precise location on Mars of the image, it could well be this was the same rectangular pattern mentioned earlier in this book, photographed by another probe. NASA did comment on it, and according to those NASA scientists, the image had probably resulted from the defrosting of the permafrost, causing it to collapse and melt. However, what might have caused this, they did not say.

Chapter Conclusion: As we have seen in this chapter, although there is still "no smoking gun" to prove aliens/Martians might still be alive on or around Mars, there is some intriguing circumstantial evidence. This includes the oddly high failure rate of craft sent to Mars (arriving at inopportune times for the aliens, and so destroyed by them—not wanting to be observed by us?), as well as the very strange photos of "something" huge in orbit near Phobos, a "something" that even cast a huge shadow onto the surface of Mars itself.

Whatever this "something" was, the Soviets of old felt it might have caused somehow the "impact" their probe suffered and so destroyed it. Either that or the probe just took that particular moment to suffer a catastrophic computer failure sending it into a permanent spin before dying completely. However, I think most of us would find that such a coincidence, although possible, was not very probable. In any case, I'm not a big fan of things just being "coincidences" under such strange circumstances. Moreover, the Soviets said something impacted the probe.

Therefore, we have two good pieces of evidence. Yes, circumstantial ones, but very intriguing ones, just the same. By the way, cylindrical objects have been photographed around other outer planets, as well. Nobody seems to know what they are, and NASA does not choose to comment on them.

Nevertheless, we conclude this chapter by saying that the very idea there might be aliens on or near Mars would mean they might not want to be exposed to us, but want to remain hidden. Therefore, the unusual high rate of failed missions to Mars, and those strange Soviet photographs might just be considered as pieces of evidence of this theory. Therefore, it is also evidence that somebody did this, and it probably wasn't humans….

Now let's move on, but still on this same topic of the idea of intelligent life possibly existing on or near Mars now. In the next chapter, we will focus on that strange moonlet, Phobos.

CHAPTER 14—Phobos A Hollow Moon?

As with our own Moon, which many have theorized might be hollow and for some of the same reasons, Phobos could well be hollow, as well. Why do so many think this? For the following reasons:

1. Phobos, as mentioned earlier, has a low density. This means it is too large for its amount of mass. Therefore, there is either missing mass or matter to make it so low density, or it is loosely held together, or as several scientists put it, "hollow."

2. Some statistics about Phobos:

Dimensions of Phobos: 27 × 22 × 18 kilometers.

Mean radius is 11.2667 kilometers.

The surface area of Phobos is 1548.3 kilometers.

Mass of Phobos is 1.0659×1016 kilograms.

Mean density of Phobos is 1.876 g/cm³.

Albedo (reflectivity) of Phobos, as mentioned earlier, is unusually low, being just 0.071±0.012.

3. Although astronomers prefer to theorize Phobos is a loosely held together pile of rubble with a thin crust binding it, this would seem highly questionable, because even those scientists can't account for how this could be, practically speaking. They have no theory as to how a thin crust could do this, hold the moon together, especially a crust that shows a long history of meteorite bombardment, with some apparently being in "chains" across the surface (another very weird oddity), and one huge one, near one of the poles of Phobos.

Such an impact should surely have exploded a loosely held pile of rubble and sent the pieces hurtling out into space in different directions, never to return. After all, the gravity of Phobos only requires an escape velocity of 41 kilometers per hour. Even a slow car could escape the surface of Phobos for good, let alone something that might have rebounded off the planet at the speed of a bullet or even higher!

4. Then there are those "chain craters" we see on the surface of Phobos, not to mention those odd "grooves," as well. The chains of craters, once thought to be the result of volcanic eruptions along fracture lines on the surface of Phobos, are almost certainly not that. Phobos is far too small to generate enough internal heat of any significance at all. It's doubtful it could warm a cup of coffee, let alone cause volcanoes to erupt.

Therefore, the moonlet couldn't possibly have had volcanic eruptions. Furthermore, neither can scientists explain why the craters are in chains or lines as they are. This means that at this point, scientists simply can't adequately account for the craters with any existing theory. So what did make them? Well, nobody seems to know for sure, but again, there are theories.

5. The "grooves" on Phobos present a similar problem for scientists. Once conjectured as being the result of other small bits of debris hitting Phobos this now doesn't seem likely, because the grooves perfectly follow the contours of the little moon, and random meteor strikes simply don't do that. Just look at close-up images of our Moon and the randomness of meteor impacts there is all too apparent.

Other scientists have wondered if they aren't some phenomenon left over from Phobos being part of a bigger body near Mars that suffered catastrophic destruction, such as a larger moon that the planet might once have had. However, this is pure conjecture with no basis in fact yet to support it in any serious way, being just another theory and one of many at that.

Hollow Phobos? Now we come to something a bit more incredible. Before the Soviet empire fell, there was an active colonel in the Soviet Air Force. This was Colonel Marina Popovich, later retired. She insisted

Phobos was hollow based on information to which she was secretly privy. She informed Steven Greer, the acting International Director of CSETI at the time of the fact that she had been informed of this by certain secret sources (Russian ones, presumably...). These sources had emphatically told her the moon, Phobos, was indeed hollow.

The strange part of this story and way back before all this information about Phobos came to light, all those missions and resulting data could not have been known because they hadn't happened yet, there was a supposed "contactee," Paul Villa Jr. He said at that time, in 1953, that an alien from a UFO had informed him Phobos was hollow.

Now, under any other circumstances, I would have grave doubts about the whole "contactee" idea, not being a fan of such things, since there is usually no evidence to support their claims at all. Still, one can't help but wonder about this particular coincidence of someone claiming they knew this decades before Colonel Popovich declared the same thing to be true. So did this supposed contactee really talk to an extraterrestrial? Alternatively, is it just a weird coincidence? Just some food for thought... .

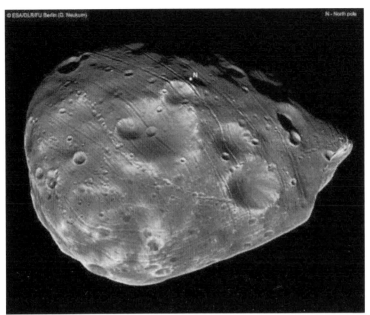

N - North pole

Photograph of Phobos with "chains of craters"
And "grooves" prominently featured.
Source: ESAVDLR/FU, Public Domain

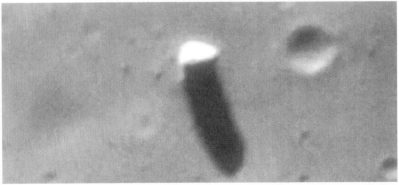

"Monolith on Phobos, building-sized or 90m tall."
Source: NASA

The implication is that Phobos isn't just "naturally hollow," but that someone hollowed it out, and the moon could well have been moved at some point to its present location. Proponents of this theory argue that the chains of craters are actually where reaction rockets were planted and set off. The idea is similar to that of the concept of the Orion nuclear spaceship, where a series of small atomic explosions propel the ship (moonlet, in this case) to velocities and distances our current chemical rockets can't dream of reaching. Setting these off on Phobos (wherever it might have been located originally), these explosions would have been done in a series making these chains of craters. This would have been in order to reposition Phobos nearer to Mars and would allow for the trajectory of the moon to be altered at will this way.

As mentioned earlier, Phobos does have an odd orbit, one that as one astronomer once put it, seems to make it "speed up and then slow down." Moreover, the orbit of Phobos isn't stable. The orbit is decaying and Phobos is, as also mentioned earlier, destined to die. Finally, some researchers estimate that Phobos may be up to one-third hollow! Phobos, it seems, is an extremely odd little moon...to odd, perhaps?

Chapter Conclusion: Although again, we do not have a "smoking gun," we are building a case for just how mysterious Mars and its moons are. Furthermore, it is a fact that the density of Phobos is just way too low. Either the moon is a loose pile of rubble held together, or alternatively, it is indeed hollow. There seem to be no other choices there.

One of the more bizarre things about the idea that Phobos could well have a hollow interior is that there is one other moon in our solar system that many claim may be just the same way. That other satellite is our own Moon. It, too, has too low a density.

Furthermore, both these moons orbit planets that have much in common with regard to one thing...either life, or the possibility of life. Earth has life, and it now seems that Mars once did, and may still harbor at least microscopic forms of it, and perhaps even more advanced forms of life, as well, perhaps hidden ones?

The coincidence of two sister worlds, each either harboring life or having harbored life in the past and both having possibly hollow moons circling them is just a bit too strange and a little too coincidental one would have to think.

Whatever the situation, if Phobos is hollow and it seems it could well be according to the available evidence, did someone deliberately hollow it out? If so, who is that "somebody?" And why did they choose a moon of Mars, or is it originally from somewhere else, perhaps the Asteroid Belt and was purposely moved into orbit around Mars? A deliberately hollowed out moon orbiting the red planet in a strange orbit would have to be considered yet another sign there might be intelligent life there.

CHAPTER 15—Aliens On Mars?

Alien life on Mars; does it really exist and did it ever? We keep asking ourselves this question. Well, as we have seen in previous chapters, Mars and its moon, Phobos, are rather strange worlds with some odd things about them. Everything from both Mars having an eccentric orbit to Phobos having a decaying orbit, to radioactive isotopes that one scientist says could well be the result of a major thermonuclear war on Mars, to a massive canyon, the Valles Marineris, which looks like the result of a huge plasma attack. Yes, odd, indeed. There is more.

Mars seems strewn with things that either resemble debris from spacecraft, for which we cannot account, as well as strange structures that look intact, and others that appear to be ancient ruins. Here are just a few of these for consideration:

This image, blurred by distance seems to show a Martian City or fortress.
Ultimate Source: NASA

The above picture shows something VERY intriguing. Look at it closely for yourself. Do you see what looks like the ruins of a hilltop fortress there? The upper left shows what appears to be a definite wall that rises (center right of picture) to a fortress-like structure. The entire top of the hill looks like this wall encloses it, and there are those semi-circular openings, half-oval shaped arches, which look as if they allow entry into the structure/wall. Is this a ruin of an ancient civilization, a fortress of old, or one that might still be used?

Are there other lifeforms on Mars, as well? Check out this photo:

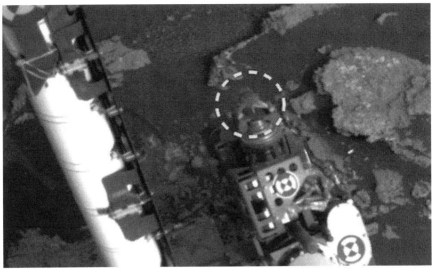

Alien lizard on NASA's Mars Rover Curiosity?
Ultimate Source: NASA

This photo was shown in "Lizard Crawling On @NASA Mars Rover This Week, March 2017," at a website by Scott C Waring. The photo taken by the Curiosity Rover itself clearly shows "something" on top of it. Furthermore, Scott Waring said that a photograph taken shortly later did not have this "something" on

Curiosity, and so it apparently left the rover by that time, meaning whatever it was, it had to have been alive?

Here is a close up of the image:

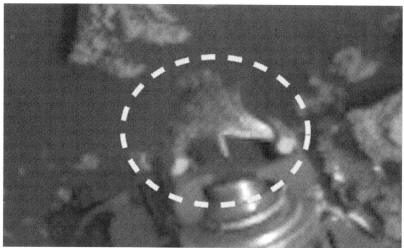

Ultimate Source: NASA

It does rather look like a lizard of some sort. Doesn't it? If not, if nothing alive, then again, how did it get on the actual Rover? Furthermore, what is it? There are also intriguing photos of other possible life forms, many of them! Everything from forests to animals of all sorts, including what looks like a migrating herd of some type of beasts, to skeletons, skulls—you name it, there are photographs of it, and these are unretouched.

Of course, with many such pictures, it takes some imagination to see what the proponents of the photos claim, but in others, the images look strikingly like what they are said to be. For instance, one of a partially buried cube looks just like that. Many more also seem to be on target in that they look very much like what some researchers and Ufologists claim them to be.

In the photo immediately below is what researchers describe as a "very large sphere" sitting on a Martian plateau. Notice the size of the shadow it casts on the ground, the shape of it? Various researchers feel this cannot be a natural feature since there seems no explanation for it being there all by itself with nothing similar around it except maybe to say it was just some odd geological formation, one of several. They have no explanation other than somebody built or put it there somehow.

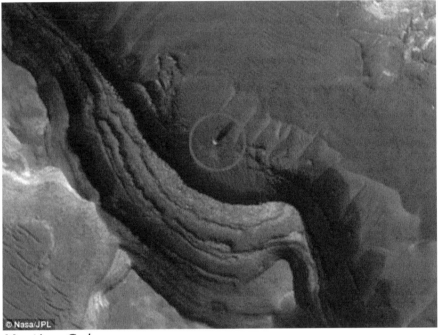

Martian Sphere
Source NASA/JPL Mars Reconnaissance Orbiter

This "bright sphere" shot was taken from the Mars Reconnaissance Orbiter. The image shows what appears to be a brightly reflective or lit sphere on the surface of Mars. The sphere is huge, as witnessed by the shadow it casts and the size it had to be to be seen from space by the Orbiter.

Now below is an image that has been sweeping the Internet and seems to show three towers, evenly spaced in a straight line across the Martian surface. In addition, as one UFO researcher put it, it looks as if they show signs of high technology and it is further claimed they are close to a mile in height!

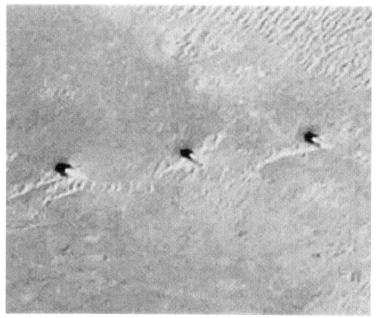

Towers on Mars?
Source Mars Global Surveyor

These towers do look as if they are truly aligned and since nothing else in the area seems to show anything similar, it is hard to imagine that these are just "natural" formations that happened to occur in such a level region otherwise, and came out so evenly spaced, as well as looking so incredibly much alike. They are all estimated to be the same in height. They all have the same weird reflective tops to them. In fact, if one looks at the one on the far left in the photograph, it almost looks like some sort of "cap" or "capsule" on the top of them. This image is of an area in a region referred to as "Terra Meridiani," and is just below the equator of Mars.

Yes, these could be natural in origin—theoretically, but ask yourself this: do they look natural? If they are, nobody seems to be able to explain how they came about, how they can all look so much like each other, how they can be so tall (and the same height), or so evenly spaced. Furthermore, they are in a flat region, with nothing like them anywhere near them, although there are several more some distance away from them. In short, they don't seem to be the result of any known geological type of activity or erosion.

Following is a picture of a "stone circle" on Mars. Some Ufologists believe this is not natural, being too much of a "perfect circle." Perhaps this is so, because it is very close to being just that a perfect circle. Therefore, such researchers believe it has to have been placed there.

However, there are two schools of thought on this issue and they contend with each other. One school says the circle looks carefully put there by "someone" perhaps in ancient times. The other school claims it is nothing more than a rather perfect ancient crater and the circle is the crumbling rim of that depression.

However, there is one slight problem with this last version. The crater isn't that large, if that's what it is. To force/melt solid rock into such a formation, it is thought that meteorite impacts must be larger in order to generate enough heat on impact to accomplish such a thing. Moreover, if it was a meteorite impact that was capable of doing this, the crater should have been much larger. In addition, there should be "rays" of debris thrown from the crater, as with Meteor Crater in Arizona here on Earth. There are not.

Of course, it is hard to tell just what the circle might be, because the rock seems to be very ancient and so is breaking up, but just an old crater rim? Possibly this is so, yet how to explain the questions about it, if this is, indeed, the case? The weird thing is that it looks like it might be in the center of an outer circle, now almost erased by time and erosion.

Martian "Stone Circle
Source: NASA, Curiosity Rover

We come now to a photo that presents a real problem for anyone who just tries to explain it away as nothing, as NASA seems to frequently try to do with so many photos. This image is of something that certainly looks artificial and it is in the sky of Mars! Not outer space, not an orbiter we've sent, nor satellite orbiting the planet, and not an incoming probe in the process of landing. In short, nobody knows what it is or what it is doing there, or how it came to be there. Here's the image:

UFO in Martian Sky? The Rover snapped this image. Source: NASA

Whatever the thing in the sky is, it does not appear to be a meteorite or anything of the sort. The object does seem to have a definite shape to it, and it almost looks rather like that of some sort of jet fighter. Alas, the picture is too fuzzy to tell.

The question has to be asked, what is it doing there? What is flying through the air on Mars? Again, this is something we have no answer for at the present time, but it is most likely something not natural, but rather artificial in nature. Just what that something is, we do not know.

Another shadow of a ship falling on Mars? For the final photo of this chapter, we come to one that just recently came to notice by a researcher who saw it on the Google Mars map. To say it is intriguing, is to put it mildly. The photo appears to be a shadow on the surface of Mars that comes from something above that surface. Here's the photo, and this is at the courtesy of Secure Team 10,

https://www.youtube.com/watch?v=B6d6wINF HbA.

Here's the shadow:

Credit: Security 10 Team, Youtube
Ultimate Source: NASA, Public Domain

Here is an image of the supposed Black Knight Satellite superimposed:

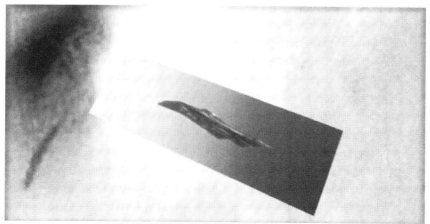

Credit: Security 10 Team, YouTube
Ultimate Source: NASA

Black Knight Satellite. This strange "satellite" has a long history. Photographed a number of times over quite a number of decades, researchers and scientists alike simply can't account for the thing. Also, a number of photographs taken at different intervals over the last 70 years or so also seem to show that something actually is "up there" and it is orbiting our world.

The whole controversey over the satellite began a long time ago, back in the 1950s at a time when as far as the humanity was concerned, nothing, and I mean nothing in the way of any kind of satellite had yet to be launched. Actually, some claim the history of the thing goes back much further. They claim that Nikola Tesla first heard the satellite "broadcasting' during radio experiments of his in 1899! Moreover, Jogen Hals, of Norway, supposedly heard the same thing as "long delayed echoes" in 1928.

Whether or not this was the Black Knight Satellite broadcasting is a matter of mystery, but in the 1950s, more was to happen. In 1954 and well before even the Soviet Union's first satellite launch of Sputnik (and well before America's, as well), Donald Keyhoe, a Ufologist, informed the news media that our military, specifically the Air Force said there were two satellites already in orbit around our planet. How this could be is yet another enigma, because supposedly, humanity hadn't launched anything in the way of anything into a permanent orbit around Earth.

Sporadic observations over the next years of "something" in orbit, a polar orbit around our planet, are mentioned, and once by the military itself. Later they said it was nothing more than a wayward satellite they had spotted, there being a number in orbit by that time. Maybe this is so, but the story wouldn't die. The thing came to be known as the "Black Knight Satellite," so named for a British project of those years, although the Black Knight is not related to it, other than the name seemed a convenient way for Ufologists to designate it.

However, the story, which had faded from public attention, was revived in 1973. Duncan Lunan, an author, decided to investigate the matter. He analyzed the radio signals that had been received by the Norwegian, Jogen Hals, along with other recordings, as well. He claimed at the time that the signals might have been as much as 13,000 years old. Later, he retracted this statement, but some say it was under duress. Once more, interest in the Black Knight Satellite waned because of this fact.

Yet, in 1998 on a NASA mission, STS-88, something was photographed that many feel was an actual image of the Black Knight itself. NASA theorized that what the picture was, was an image of a "thermal blanket" that had been lost on an extravehicular activity, but this was never confirmed in a real way. Suggesting it "might" be something, certainly doesn't make it so. Below is a picture of the object. Decide for yourself if this looks anything like a "thermal blanket..."

Black Knight Satellite?
Source: NASA

As always with such things, controversy rages over what this object is. The fact that it seems to have all sorts of protuberances and reflects light on some of them, seems to indicate a hard, rigid object that is metallic in nature and that reflects sunlight in some areas. It certainly seems to bear no resemblance to a "thermal blanket." The fact that when first reported back in the mid-fifties, the object was said to have been in a polar orbit (which nobody had ever done then—again, not having even launched any satellites yet), is also strange. Finally, the shape of the object is almost a perfect match for the "shadow" seen on Mars in earlier photographs in this book.

As an odd side note, Astronaut Buzz Aldrin, after his recent trip to Antarctica at the South Pole, was claimed to have tweeted that we were all in danger ("humanity"), and that something he referred to as an "it" was in fact, "evil itself." This tweet disappeared, deleted, apparently.

The fact the Black Knight orbits Earth in a polar orbit means that periodically, it is right over Antarctica and the South Pole. Just a coincidence? Perhaps, but then again, perhaps not.... Of course, controversies swirl around if this tweet really happened, again as always seems to be the case. Yet, Buzz Aldrin did take that strange trip to Antarctica in a time span when other very notable people from around the world did, as well, and nobody seems to know why they went there. Why were trips to Antarctica, all in the same year, suddenly so popular? Aldrin is also known for being outspoken about things he has seen and done, including having made references to UFOs.

In any case, what does this mean with regard to the strange satellite? Could there be more than one Black Knight, one orbiting Mars, as well, as it does our world? Alternatively, does "our" Black Knight Satellite have the ability to maneuver through space to another planet such as Mars? In the early articles on the topic, it does mention the thing was difficult to track because it could change its orbit and location, seemingly at will, and so had to have been something "artificial" in order to do this. Whatever it is, the Black Knight Satellite seems to be an enduring mystery, and now in not only Earth orbit, but perhaps in Mars orbit, as well? Yet another mystery...

Weird lights on Mars. Something else of note is the weird lights seen by our rovers on Mars. These seem to come from the ground up and create incredible glows in highly localized areas, almost as if they were jets of light. Nobody seems to know what they are and what could cause them, although NASA has made a number of "suggestions" but with no evidence at all to support any of them. Therefore, they are, in short, just that, suggestions or possible hypotheses of what the lights might be. The lights do not seem to be volcanic in nature, since there is no sign of any sort of such activity in the areas where these have been photographed. Nor do they in any way resemble any form of lightning we know of. Here is an image of one such light:

One of a number of weird lights or "glows" on the Martian surface.
Image Source: Google Mars Map

Train tracks on Mars? If this isn't enough to make one wonder about life being on Mars now—intelligent life that is, here's a Google Mars Map image and this one is most definitely hard to explain any other way. It is often referred to as "train tracks." Please see the picture below.

As you can see, there is no known "natural" way these could have gotten there as yet, and the fact it looks like there is not only something like a depot or station of sorts right near the tracks, but in one picture, it looks like something is actually on the tracks. Notice there is no sign of those things being open in any way to the Martian atmosphere? They look sealed or self-contained. Moreover, the tracks are very evenly spaced and look VERY artificial. Images:

Source: Google Mars Map
Credit: Alfred Snyder for spotting this image.

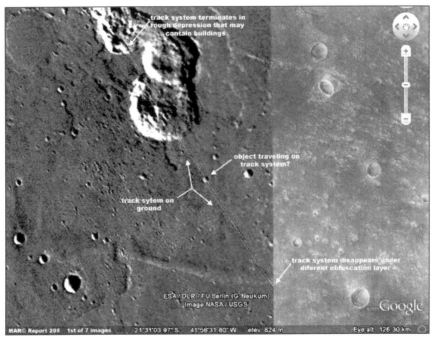

Source: Mars Anomaly Research, NASA, Public Domain
Credit:
http://www.marsanomalyresearch.com/evidenc
e-directories/8-book/book-directory.htm

This is an interesting version of the same photo because it shows what some researchers think we might be seeing. Furthermore, it shows how the track "disappears" the next image over ("obfuscation in adjacent image"). Whatever the tracks are, it should be remember that "nature abhors straight lines," and these lines are just about as straight and evenly spaced as one can get. So if not artificially made, how could they be reasonably accounted for? The answer is, as of now, they can't be. An alien railroad? It just might be one of sorts.

Chapter Conclusion: We have seen in this chapter that there are definitely a number of anomalies on the surface of Mars and yes, even in its skies. The photo of the "UFO" in the Martian skies is particularly intriguing, along with some of the other photos, as well, including the Black Knight Satellite "shadow" on Mars, because that shadow is in the exact shape of the supposed Black Knight Satellite. There are many more such "anomalies," in fact, the planet seems to be littered with them, not only on its surface, but now in its skies, as well.

Nevertheless, what are we to make of all of this? Certainly, some of the images are so blurred as to rule out any certainty one way or the other. Others could be natural formations, albeit, very odd ones. The only thing we can say for sure is that these are the original NASA and ESA photos, unretouched (as used in this book).

Yet other images are downright intriguing, as with the UFO photo by the Rover, and the one of those "towers." Again, there are many more such photos of "anomalous structures" on Mars, including domes, pyramids, what appear to be more ruins, etc.

However, none of these can definitively prove that Martians did exist or now exist on Mars, although they certainly and strongly tease us about the idea. Even if one accepts that most photos of anomalies on Mars are just odd natural formations, there are still some that do defy this description.

Still, is there other evidence that might also contribute to the idea that "someone" is on Mars, or very near the planet, say in the interior of Phobos? Or are we just left with wondering if there could be advanced life, intelligent life with no further data to confirm whether it exists or not?

Although the photographs presented here do stir one's imagination in this regard, they are, again, not definitive proof of intelligent life by themselves. Therefore, to answer the question about intelligent life on Mars, we must backtrack just a bit, and first have to ascertain if the likelihood of advanced life outside of our own species might even exist at all, anywhere. In the next chapter, we will look into this possibility/probability.

CHAPTER 16—Does Alien Intelligence Exist At All?

If one is to entertain the idea that intelligent Martians might exist, one first has logically to agree to the premise that aliens of such a nature exist at all...anywhere.

Do we have such evidence for the existence of extraterrestrials?

Again, the short answer in my estimation is a resounding yes! We do. In addition, lots of it. This evidence, as I've shown in other books, is everywhere and virtually all pervasive. Pick a source and you can find evidence for the idea that extraterrestrials exist.

Of course, many will say that NASA doesn't support the idea that there is any such evidence *("at present")* for such a statement. No? Well, many of their astronauts and employees do!

Remember, these same people did all the dangerous work for NASA in that they went into space, went to the Moon and back, and helped to build the ISS platform now orbiting Earth. So NASA trusts them for that, but then ignores what they have to say about seeing extraterrestrials while "out there?" Nor is it just "one or two" astronauts claiming this. There are a number of them, as well as other employees of NASA, all who have declared UFOs real. Here's a short list of those that do:

Edgar Mitchell. One who walked on the moon (the sixth astronaut to do this), had repeatedly, clearly, and loudly insisted that:

"...aliens have contacted humans several times."

Commander Eugene Cernan. In an L.A. Times piece, he said:

"...I've been asked (about UFOs) and I've said publicly I thought they were somebody else, some other civilization."

Major Gordon Cooper. He has repeatedly espoused the fact that UFOs and extraterrestrials exist. He even went in front of a United Nations committee and emphatically stated that one of the astronauts had actually witnessed a UFO on the ground.

Donald Slayton. An astronaut in the original Mercury Program (which predated the Gemini and Apollo series), when once interviewed, stated that as long ago as 1951, while test piloting an aircraft:

"I was testing a P-51 fighter in Minneapolis when I spotted this object. I was at about 10,000 feet on a nice, bright, sunny afternoon. I thought the object was a kite, then I realized that no kite is gonna fly that high…. As I got closer, it looked like a weather balloon, gray, and about three feet in diameter. But as soon as I got behind the darn thing it didn't look like a balloon anymore. It looked like a saucer, a disk. About the same time, I realized that it was suddenly going away from me—and there I was, running at about 300 miles per hour. I tracked it for a little way, and then all of a sudden the damn thing just took off. It pulled about a 45-degree climbing turn and accelerated and just flat disappeared."

Joseph A. Walker. In 1962 Joseph Walker, already then a NASA pilot declared that one of his jobs while taking the X-15 spy flights was also to photograph UFOs. He said that he had actually filmed "five or six" such UFOs during a 50-mile flight above the Earth in April of 1962. Nor was he reticent about what he had seen. During a lecture at the Second National

Conference on the Peaceful Uses of Space Research in Seattle, he said:

"I don't feel like speculating about them. All I know is what appeared on the film which was developed after the flight."

None of the films have ever been released to the public.

Major Robert White. Pilot Joseph Walker wasn't the only one to see things while test piloting an X-15. July 17, 1962, then Major White reported witnessing an unidentified flying object while on a 58-mile high mission in his X-15. In his report, he stated:

"I have no idea what it could be. It was grayish in color and about thirty to forty feet away."

The story doesn't quite end there. Time Magazine, in an article, stated that Major White had also said while broadcasting his report that:

"There are things out there! There absolutely is!"

James Lovell and Frank Borman. In 1965, these two astronauts witnessed a UFO while in orbit about the Earth. Specifically, Borman said he could see an unidentified object or craft, which Kennedy Spaceport said might be the booster rocket from their own launch. Borman denied this immediately, saying he could also see the booster rocket, as well. It was in plain sight. Lovell had originally reported the UFO as a "bogey."

Edwin Aldrin. Fellow astronaut with Neil Armstrong when they landed on the Moon with Apollo 11 said they were supposedly "warned off" the Moon by extraterrestrials.

Maurice Chatelain. One-time chief of NASA Communications Systems; he reported that Neil Armstrong had most definitely reported the fact that two alien spacecraft had been sighted perched on the edge of a crater overlooking the Apollo 11 landing site.

As he put it:

"The encounter was common knowledge in NASA, but nobody has talked about it until now."

He further stated that:

"...all Apollo and Gemini flights were followed, both at a distance and sometimes also quite closely, by space vehicles of extraterrestrial origin—flying saucers, or UFOs, if you want to call them by that name. Every time it occurred, the astronauts informed Mission Control, who then ordered absolute silence."

He even further went on to say that:

"I think that Walter Schirra aboard Mercury 8 was the first of the astronauts to use the code name 'Santa Claus' to indicate the presence of flying saucers next to space capsules."

However, his announcements were barely noticed by the public. It was a little different when James Lovell on board the Apollo 8 command module came out from behind the moon and said for everybody to hear:

"Please be informed that there is a santa claus."

To corroborate his statement, we have the evidence also provided by Otto Binder and Dr. Garry Henderson, who also declared that all NASA personnel, specifically astronauts, were under command to never repeat any information about their having witnessed UFOs.

Neil Armstrong. First man to walk on the Moon supposedly stated to a professor once that the Aliens would appear to have bases on the Moon, and went on to say thatthey were "told" to stay off the Moon. He further added that this was the reason the astronauts stayed so briefly, "just a scoop" and return mission, as it were.

James McDivit and Ed White. June 1965, both astronauts James McDivitt and Ed White were in orbit when they spotted and photographed a UFO. It appeared "metallic" to them. NASA has never released the photographs of this object, not then and not now.

Scott Carpenter. He said:

"At no time, when the astronauts were in space were they alone: there was a constant surveillance by UFOs."

This list doesn't even include the more "rank and file" members of NASA and related agencies who also claim they have seen proof that extraterrestrials exist. That list is a long one. It includes people who have seen NASA subcontractors airbrushing out evidence on photographs before releasing them to the public, or witnessed gatherings of international authorities to discuss the "extraterrestrial question," or military personnel on military bases, such as Edwards Air force Base who claim to have seen UFO landings, there, etc.

Moreover, I haven't even included all the police, military pilots, commercial pilots, and civilian authorities who claim to have witnessed, firsthand, evidence that aliens exist. Even presidents have witnessed UFOs:

Presidents Jimmy Carter and Ronald Regan. Both claimed to have seen UFOs prior to becoming president.

Arizona Governor Fife Symington. He was governor of Arizona from 1990 to 1998. Only after he left office did he declare that he was a witness "to one of the world's biggest ever mass UFO sightings." Furthermore, he unequivocally declared he thought the lights were extraterrestrial in nature.

This is in direct contradiction to what he said at the time the event occurred as governor, when he had a walk-on at one of his press conferences with a man in a ridiculous alien costume. He explained that at the time, he felt the whole thing was getting dangerously out of hand, and he wanted to avoid a public panic, so he did what so many other officials have done, deliberately lied and/or dismissed/ridiculed the whole event. That is until he was no longer governor. Freed at last of such political constraints, he felt able at last to "come out" and declare what it was really all about.

Now, I am not bothering to include the countless civilians (now in the millions) who have also seen UFOs, or claim to have experienced abductions by extraterrestrials. That list is a VERY long one! There just is no room for it here, of course. So it goes and continues to go.

Videos and photographs in their thousands for decades and still coming forth, testimonials of people on their deathbeds or after they've retired from military or political life, testimony of former governors, such as the governor of Arizona during the infamous Phoenix Lights event, and even presidents have all said the same thing. They have seen UFOs, or UFOs exist and/or extraterrestrials exist.

In fact, the testimonies to this idea of UFOs and extraterrestrials existing being true are legion, so legion; in fact, that I won't even attempt to argue that this is more proof of the existence of alien lifeforms. More testimonies won't make those who simply choose not to believe, change their minds. Some simply don't want it to be true. They are afraid and perhaps rightly so of what it all might mean for us humans.

If the statements of many of NASA's own astronauts and NASA personnel, as listed above, who actually held high positions in NASA, went to space, flew to the moon and back aren't enough for such people, then really, what would be? Apparently, not even the statements of former governors or presidents is enough to sway their intransigence in this matter. Denial is their watchword of the day.

However, denial at some point just becomes ridiculous. As a MUFON Field Investigator and prior to that, as a decades-long investigator on my own, I've seen ample evidence of "something" taking place in our skies, seas, and on land, and that "something" doesn't seem to be us! The interviews I've had with countless respectable citizens as witnesses to such events, including among them biochemists, professors, and law enforcement personnel, long ago convinced me that something is going on, and whatever it is, it is big!

Either one accepts the incredible preponderance of evidence for this being a fact, or one never will, I suppose. One cannot force the truth upon someone. They simply have to accept it for themselves, or not, as the case may be.

Yet, the truth is simple. Millions have witnessed UFOs. Thousands have had to (like it or not) interact with them. People the world over have had property damaged by such interactions.

Some people have been sickened and injured in such dealings. Worse, a number of people have died from such contacts, including military and civilians in the USA and around the world. If nothing is out there, then who killed and injured these people? Who damaged their property? I assure you, it wasn't just swamp gas, that old and silly excuse put forth during the old Project Blue Book days to explain away UFOs.

Leaving aside the whole question of abductions, I'm just talking here about verifiable facts. For more information on this, please see my book, *Deadly UFOS And The Disappeared* (please see References section for link) where I list many of the major cases of just these sorts of interactions with UFOs and describe them in detail. There are dozens of other books by other authors on the same subject, as well, so I'm hardly a voice "crying in the wilderness" on this topic.

Chapter Conclusion: One could go on for literally thousands upon thousands of pages in supplying testimonies and eyewitness accounts of UFOs and/or extraterrestrials. I have quite a number of books on the subject, for instance, and again, there are many, many such books by other researchers/authors, as well.

One more time: people have witnessed UFOs in the hundreds of thousands, at least. People have seen their property damaged by UFO encounters. People have been sickened by UFO encounters. People have died in UFO encounters, and far more often than one might think. This includes military pilots and personnel, as well as civilians, and not only in the United States, but round the world.

Practically no country has gone untouched by the UFO phenomenon to one degree or another. Nor are these just a current phenomenon, but date back to the 1950s, with many arguing (myself included) such events have occurred throughout our history, centuries and even millennia ago. As just one example of this, check out this photograph of an infamous renaissance painting:

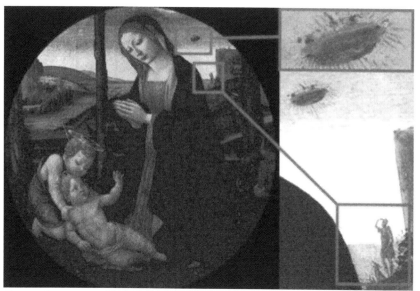

Renaissance Painting with UFO in Background and Man Peering up at it.
Source: Credit Proof Of Aliens Life/Public Domain

At the time such paintings were done, it was normal for the artists to include things people had seen in the skies at the time that were odd or different, because they thought of them as manifestations of the heaven and the divine. In this famous painting, the man is obviously peering up into the sky at the object. Nor does the object look like anything heavenly or "divine." In fact, it very much resembles a rather spikey looking UFO in every aspect! Finally, this isn't the only such painting. There are many of this sort, but this is certainly one of the more profound ones, and so has become famous in this regard, or rather, infamous!

Whatever that thing is in the skies, it certainly couldn't have been manmade, not back then, for not even hot air balloons had been discovered at that point, and certainly nothing that resembled the painting of that UFO!

However, with the advent of the photographic camera, and its sudden spread in the form of cellphones around the world, many more photos are now being taken of UFOs. Until the last century, we had to rely strictly on people's testimony to these events, and/or drawings or painting they did of them, like the one above. Now with the phone camera becoming so ubiquitous photographic evidence of UFOs is flooding us.

Are some of these photos hoaxed? Of course. There is always that element that for some reason or other, mostly to gain notoriety, are willing to hoax these events. But when they are seen by groups of people, even up and into the thousands at one time and in real time, the chances of such evidence being hoaxed pretty much disappears.

Therefore, if UFOs have been around for centuries, and certainly the last 70 years or so, at the very least, and they fly in ways that astound our knowledge of the sciences and technology involved, then they can't be "ours." Furthermore, if not "ours," then they have to be "theirs." It's that simple. Moreover, by "theirs" I mean those who are not human, but rather extraterrestrials.

This is a matter of simple logic and the result of using the Principle of Occam's Razor, that principle so used by scientists everywhere. No matter how one looks at it, extraterrestrials seem to exist. And if they exist here and have such advanced technologies, what makes us think that they don't exist elsewhere, or can fly wherever they want to, including such places as Mars?

Given all the witness accounts by our astronauts and everyone, including governors and presidents, given the photographs, and yes, even those paintings of old, it would appear that extraterrestrial intelligence does exist and has for a very long time.

For me, again, the evidence is overwhelming. There is a preponderance of evidence to support the idea UFOs exist. This evidence has been coming in for decades in this respect, and many of the sources are just too reliable to ignore, as the government so frequently tries to make us do.

Therefore, for me, personally, the verdict is in, and it is that extraterrestrials of some sort do exist. Their origins are a mystery, but the fact of their existence is real. Either that or several military officials and civilians in their deathbed confessions have lied, numerous astronauts have done the same, as have other military and civilian officials around the world.

Since I find such a thing even harder to believe, that there could be such a worldwide conspiracy to hoax evidence for the existence of UFOs by such reliable and trained observers, I have again to ascribe to the idea that extraterrestrials do exist. There is "something" in our skies.

Moreover, that "something" is not us. Worse, whoever "they" are, we don't seem (at least the average person doesn't) to know why they are here. Perhaps our government or governments do. Certainly, they seem actively involved in dismissing the idea or covering things up, despite the evidence of so many trained professionals, and yes, even presidents and governors, as well.

Of course, it is for each of us to decide whether we believe all this evidence or not. For me, it is no longer a matter of belief, but rather, a matter of reality. UFOs exist. Ergo, extraterrestrials exist. Additionally, they seem to have a technology we can't begin to match, and yes, that's frightening, of course. Furthermore, it gives rise to all sorts of conspiracy theories, some of which just might be true, as we shall see in the next section of this book.

PART VII—MARS AND THE WORLD OF CONSPIRACIES

CHAPTER 17—Secret Space Fleets?

Among conspiracy theories involving Mars, one of the most pervasive and long-lasting ones is that there is a secret space fleet in our solar system. As with researcher and UFO hunter, Gary Mckinnon, who claimed spacecraft have been coming and going on a regular basis from at least one United States Air Force base for at least three or more years now (with some film to back his contention), many other researchers also claim much the same thing. They point to evidence that has come from a number of sources. Gary McKinnon even has a name for this supposed secret space fleet, and that is, "Solar Warden."

Why is this important to us when we are talking about Mars? Well, if there actually is some sort of space fleet, human or alien, that could account for what the Russians with their Fobos 2 mission ran into near the red planet. It might also account for some of the many other failed missions to Mars, as well. If they don't want to be seen, then it would be easy enough to destroy incoming probes that might spot them in such a manner. Finally, it might account for some of those many anomalies seen on Mars, such as the weird glowing lights, the "railroad tracks," the metallic domes, those strange mile-high towers, etc. So, let's look at some of this evidence for a secret space fleet and see if it holds up at all.

Spacecraft at Nellis Air Force Base? There is another UFO researcher by the name of Steven Barone. On his YouTube channel, he makes the claim that UFOs of an extraterrestrial source, or at the very least, secret American spacecraft, have been seen hovering over Nellis Air Force Base in Nevada.

This base is not to be confused with Area 51, which is not far from there, and is actually instead considered a part of Edwards Air Force Base. Nellis Air Force Base is huge and originally was well out of the Las Vegas area, although that city has since grown and now sprawls to the very edge of the base in some places.

Actually, I lived on Nellis Boulevard in Las Vegas in the mid-1970s. It was a common thing for people living in that area to claim to have seen strange lights as a regular occurrence over the nearby base, so on this one piece of evidence, I'm a bit biased, because I have seen just this sort of thing twice myself, while living there. Steven also shows films on his YouTube site that reveal some of these same weird lights, and their even weirder behavior.

As mentioned, Area 51 isn't so very far away from Nellis and it has long been held as an area where secret craft, again many say alien in origin, are supposed to be located. Once more, I have personal knowledge of this, as well. My brother, who experienced missing time as a teenager, along with a close friend of his (and no, they do not claim to have been abducted, since they have no memory of what happened that night), developed an avid interest in Area 51 because of this.

He personally videotaped some very weird lights darting in impossible ways (according to the known laws of physics) above Area 51. That is, he did until the government exercised rights of eminent domain and seized the mountaintop from which he and his friends, as well as others were filming.

What does all this mean? Well, something of a unique nature does definitely seem to be going on at these bases. Furthermore, that "something" seems to defy the laws of physics, as we know them. For example, the incredible speeds and sudden stops would liquefy any passengers aboard such craft, unless somehow the Law of Inertia is circumvented. These spacecraft may be able to go at impossible speeds and stop on a dime, but the occupants wouldn't be able to,

182

and so should come to an abrupt and messy end under such circumstances, splattered onto the nearest bulkhead. However, they don't seem to....

What's more, all this involves the sighting of weird lights in the sky that seem capable of doing these incredible maneuvers. In short, because we don't know what they are, and/or can't identify them, then they are technically UFOs. This means that either "we" or perhaps "they" have some extraordinary capabilities with regard to some sort of flying technology. Regardless of whose craft they might be, it means somebody has such incredible vehicles. Even that on its own is a fascinating thing to know.

Holloman Air Force Base, 1973. Two men, Allan Sandler and Robert Emengger were making a documentary. In the film was included a short segment on an extraordinary topic, UFOs and extraterrestrials. The segment supposedly had been filmed by the military in 1971, just two years before, and it was of an alien craft landing at Holloman Air Force Base, New Mexico.

During the filming of the documentary, the military showed Robert Emengger an area there at the base where aliens and humans met to communicate. Moreover, they informed him this hadn't been a first contact occasion with the aliens, since government officials had met with these creatures before.

Furthermore, Robert Emenegger said he had been informed that the government had been monitoring another alien group, as well, and that part of this conference was to see if these aliens (who landed at Holloman) knew anything about these other ones. The Holloman aliens disavowed all knowledge of any other species at the time.

The documentary was released the following year in 1974. *UFOs: Past, Present and Future* was the title, and although it only contained a very short segment of the landing of the aliens at Holloman, it did show some. The film, later inspected by experts, was deemed not to have been faked or altered.

Gary McKinnon. A young Scots hacker, he managed to hack his way into NASA's computer systems at the Johnson Space Center in Texas. His intent wasn't malicious, in that he didn't wish to damage or destroy anything, or to steal information for espionage purposes. Instead, he simply wanted to know if he could find out anything about UFOs that NASA might be hiding.

To his surprise, he found something inconceivable, something he had no idea existed, or so he claims. He discovered (according to him) that "out there" was a secret space fleet. This space fleet, according to a document he saw, had been created in the early 1980's. This fleet, composed of eight to ten large ships ("tubular" in shape) also had close to 50 other ones, as well. When he later tried to publicly search for these ships by their names, he could find nothing, which further confirmed for him they were part of a hidden fleet.

Furthermore, and this surprised him even more, there was also a roster of officers, which, apparently, included "non-terrestrial officers." Many assume this to mean that there were aliens included aboard these vessels, but one must also consider that "non-terrestrial officers" might simply mean humans not stationed on Earth. These, too, could be considered "non-terrestrial." To go even further, McKinnon claimed the space fleet's base of operations was at Area 51, and Nellis Air Force Base.

What we do know about all this is that Mr. McKinnon did hack into NASA and the United States military's computers. The U.S. government has waged an ongoing campaign to have McKinnon extradited from the United Kingdom, but have been thwarted in this.

Therefore, we know that McKinnon did break into NASA's computers, and undoubtedly saw things he wasn't supposed to have seen. Just what those things really were, is hard to say, since only McKinnon saw them. However, he does stand by his statements.

Moreover, the ferocity with which the U.S. government has tried to extradite him from the United Kingdom shows just how serious and angry they were over the matter. The penalty for what McKinnon did could be as much as 60 to 70 years in jail and up to two million dollars (or more) in fines. This means McKinnon went to extraordinary lengths to find information and at a potentially great cost to himself. Therefore, it seems reasonable he is telling the truth about what he found, or at the very least, as he perceived the truth to be.

Captain Kaye. Gary McKinnon is not alone in his claims of a secret space fleet. A man, who wished to remain anonymous as a whistleblower, and who goes by the appellation, "Captain Kaye," but who since has been revealed as being Randy Cramer, has also claimed the same thing. He states that he actually served in the space fleet and that the fleet was an international one run by the "Earth Defense Force."

Captain Kaye claims other things, as well:

1. He was recruited by the Special Section of the United States Marines, a secret branch of the Corps to become a member of the Space Fleet. He states that he served a total of 20 years in the fleet and was stationed for most of that time on Mars.

2. He claims others from various military organizations around the world also were recruited for the Space Fleet and this includes our supposed enemies, Russia and China.

3. Kaye also insists that there were colonies on Mars, all human, and it was part of his job to guard them against native Martian life forms. This, apparently, included intelligent beings, as well as guarding against some types of dangerous animals.

4. Captain Kaye stated there were three main types of ships used as space fighters, and three types of bomber craft, as well. These ships used various means of propulsion, including fission and fusion drives (as with the "Orion" idea for a spaceship), as well as some means of propulsion he referred to as "electro-gravitic" that seems to have been some type of anti-gravity drive. Bob Lazar, former (confirmed) physicist, who claims to have worked at Area 51 also mentioned such a drive.

5. Kaye was assigned to training on the Moon at a base referred to as Lunar Operations Command, but also he spent time on or near the moon Titan of Saturn, as well as also having been trained in interplanetary deep space.

6. Kaye stated that while in service, one was completely cut off from personal communications to Earth and any information he and other crewmembers were given was on a strictly "need to know" basis.

7. Captain Kaye also stated that the space fleet included five interstellar craft that were carriers for the smaller ships and that these had the capability of traveling to the stars. His ship was supposedly the "EDF SS Nautilus," which he claims was close to three quarters of a mile in length. If so, it was a truly massive ship!

8. Kaye also stated that he had been recruited as a teenager, and upon being released from the service, found himself back on Earth in 1987, the year he had first been recruited, and that he had been age-reversed engineered to being a teenager again. Only fifteen minutes or so had passed while he had spent 20 years in the Space Fleet.

This is, of course, an astounding claim, this being in a space fleet, stationed on Mars, and then most of all, age reversed and sent back in time. Still, one the interesting parts about all this is that although, Captain Kaye's claims seem "way out there," they actually are very consistent with the claims of others. For example, he isn't the only whistleblower to have claimed this:

Corey Goode. Corey Goode also states that he, too, served for 20 years and like Cramer/Kaye, he went to Mars, as well. He also makes the same astounding claim that he was then age reversed and sent back to the time he had been first recruited. This means that two people, independently, have made the same fantastic claim.

Michael Relf. Then there is Michael Relf. His is another who insists very much the same thing happened to him, and that he, too, had a 20-year stint where he served on Mars, and again, he also was age reversed and then sent back to 1976, when he had been first recruited. Relf states that part of his stint in the service was to help establish two colonies on Mars.

Various aerospace engineers, experts, and others have revealed certain aspects of secret technologies our government supposedly has at its disposal, including technologies that involve antigravity. As Ben Rich, a former CEO of Lockheed Skunkworks once claimed, we can:

"take ET home."

President Regan. Moreover, Ronald Reagan, former president of the United States, on June 11, 1985, made an entry in his diary in which he stated:

"Lunch with 5 top space scientist. It was fascinating. Space truly is the last frontier and some of the developments there in astronomy, etc. are like science fiction, except they are real. I learned that our shuttle capacity is such that we could orbit 300 people."

At no time, supposedly, did our tiny fleet of space shuttles, even combined, ever come close to being able to carry 300 people into orbit at one time. In fact, the most any one shuttle could manage would have been eight people. For the President of the United States to claim otherwise and on such a scale is an eye-opening revelation, indeed!

Was President Reagan in this diary entry referring to the fact that a secret space fleet was in coming into existence? If our shuttles, the whole fleet combined, could only carry 40 people at most, then how, as many as 300 people, could be lofted into space at one time? Supposedly, we didn't have the ships to come close to carrying so many people. Therefore, many say this is a direct allusion to the program, Solar Warden. Because if not Solar Warden, then just how were so many hundreds of people supposed to get into space at one time?

Solar Warden, again, is apparently the name of the hidden space fleet, and of course, "solar warden" implies the fleet is protecting our solar system. Some whistleblowers say those corporations that work in U.S. government black projects primarily compose the fleet. However, they also get help from other countries. The exact nature of this organization, how it runs, and who ultimately controls it is still a matter of conjecture.

Of course, despite all this tantalizing evidence, the actual physical reality of the secret space fleet is still in question, since we have no other evidence, then these statements by a former president, various whistleblowers, for that matter many other whistleblowers, as well, that the fleet really exists. Or do we? Actually, we well may have.

Spaceships using sun to refuel? Recent images taken of the sun by NASA have had some very odd things appear in them. What looks like craft sucking plasma from the sun can be seen in some of the pictures. Moreover, several pictures were obviously pixelated to block out "something" in them, and this pixilation was by NASA, itself, it seems, since they were there when released by that organization to its website. Below are several images of this sort of thing:

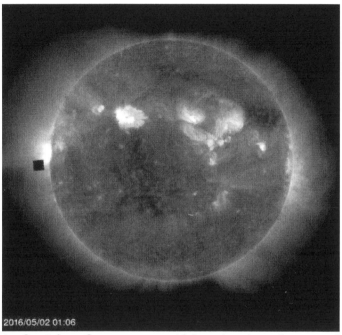

Left side of sun, something in the shape of a cube, or something pixelated out.
Source: NASA, Public Domain

Some type of craft hovering above the sun?
Source: Daily Mail, UK, Ultimate Source:
NASA,Public Domain

Distant View of Same Craft above sun
Source: Daily Mail, UK, Ultimate Source: NASA,
Public Domain

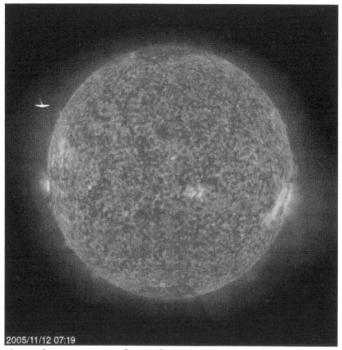
Another type of craft near top left side of sun?
Source: NASA, Public Domain

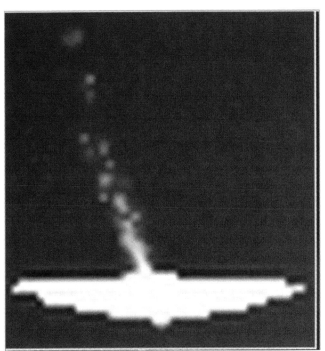

Close-up image of spacecraft on left side of sun
Source: NASA, Public Domain

The interesting part about this NASA photo is that no sooner was this image noticed and released on YouTube, then NASA, the next day, declared that they had to do an "emergency Sun reacquisition mode." This meant they had to shut down the transmission from the satellite.

Furthermore, the object is definitely not "meteor shaped," and it seems to be emitting an exhaust plume of some sort. And no, this is most definitely not a comet, either, so just what is it? You decide for yourself. As for me, it appears too symmetrical to be natural, the shape too odd to be a comet or meteor.

Secret space shuttle. Now we come to something that is also very odd. Most Americans are aware of the secret military space shuttle, although the news media barely seems to cover stories about it much, probably because they simply don't have any access to the top-secret project. However, the purpose of this military space shuttle, or rather top-secret spaceplanes (there are two known to exist, at least) is a complete mystery.

The spaceplane, or mini space shuttle is referred to as the X-37B and flies without a crew, being more like a drone in this respect than a spaceship for humans. One of the recent flights lasted almost two years and the spaceplane flew in low Earth orbit all that time...supposedly. There have been at least three flights of the two spaceplanes prior to this one. Upon its return from that flight, Brigadier General Wayne Monteith said:

"Our team has been preparing for this event for several years, and I am extremely proud to see our hard work and dedication culminate in today's safe and successful landing of the X-37B."

The ship flew for about 700 days. By the way, Brigadier General Wayne Monteith is the commander of the Air Force's Space Wing, which in itself was a surprise, because most people had never heard of the Space Wing of the Air Force. Even more were surprised the space plane had been orbiting overhead for so long a time! The Brigadier General, of course, did not say why it was up there so long, or what the purpose of the mission was. The nature of that was top secret. However, the military did say with regard to the spaceplanes that their purpose was to:

"...demonstrate technologies for a reliable, reusable, unmanned space test platform."

The idea of using such drone-like space vehicles was the result of NASA and the government wishing to come up with a cheaper form of space travel. However, what started out as a NASA project in 1998, was then turned over to the military completely, and then came under the even more secretive jurisdiction of DARPA, or the Defense Advanced Research Agency. No more news of any significance about the project was forthcoming at that point.

The spaceplanes, which again, do resemble much smaller versions of the space shuttles, but had some major differences besides there smaller sizes, as well. For one thing, they only way about 11,000 pounds. For another, they use a modified heat shield, not the same as the one used by the shuttles.

So what do we know about what the spaceplanes are for? Well, if the military is to be believed in this matter (and why shouldn't we believe them...right?), then one of the purposes of a particular flight was to test the efficacy of some type of a propulsion system, one electrical in nature. They also claimed they were testing the results of what happened to various materials in virtually zero gravity.

Other than that, everything else is pure guesswork. Some argue the ship is testing whether they can use it to approach satellites and either repair, modify, or destroy them, as in being a satellite killer. Others counter this by saying it would be far cheaper merely to make a satellite capable of taking out other satellites and launch those, instead. Perhaps, the spaceplane carried such satellites aboard it to dispense them into orbits at appropriate points for targeting other countries' satellites "for the kill." Nobody knows for sure.

Others speculate that the spaceplanes just are used to check out other countries' satellites up close, to spy on their technological capabilities, so to speak. In any case, one can name it, and there is someone there who thinks the spaceplane might be used for such a purpose, including interacting with a hidden space fleet.

Of course, along with being top secret, the space planes' cost is also a closely guarded secret, as well. We do know that between NASA and the Air Force that some $125 million had been allocated to develop the spaceplanes originally, and that Boeing later added some $67 million to this amount, but was then reimbursed later to the tune of some $301 million. Still, that's about all we do know for sure. Again, everything else about this top-secret project is kept very hush-hush.

One of the problems with the spaceplane really is for what real purpose it was built. Anything that the military said it was sent up to do, and why that one trip should last almost two years, if so, is a mystery, can also be done by sending up regular types of satellites at a far cheaper cost. So exactly, why do they have the spaceplanes?

Again, we simply don't know. The spaceplane is too like a space shuttle in that it is not highly and quickly maneuverable, so would make a poor space fighter. Again, other types of missions could fulfill its stated supposed functions much more cheaply and easily, as with Space-X sending its unscrewed rockets to the ISS to resupply those aboard that station.

What one does wonder is if the spaceplane wasn't really in orbit for 700 days, or at least not all of that time. What if it was taken aboard a bigger ship of the Space Warden fleet and then taken elsewhere, perhaps even to the Moon or Mars for some purpose? This is pure conjecture on my part, of course, but one does definitely wonder why a spaceplane would be up in space for almost two years! One also wonders what advantages a spaceplane would have over much cheaper robotic missions, such as Space-X is using...

Chapter Conclusion: As amazing as all this may sound about the idea of a secret space fleet and or a fleet of alien vessels, as well as secret government spaceplanes, etc., might be, it is odd that a number of entirely independent sources have claimed this, the idea of a secret fleet. It is further strange that then President Reagan made a notation in his diary about meeting with scientists who informed him they had the capability of sending 300 people at one time into space when our shuttle capabilities only allowed for 40 or so, maximum.

If true, this could account for the strange sightings of objects in space near Mars, and near other planets, as well, for that matter. It was either our fleet, or "theirs," perhaps?

Of course, as with all such conspiracy theories, one must view them with a very skeptical eye, and yet in this case of a secret space fleet, there are intriguing factors about it.

First, we have a young hacker, so interested in UFOs that he hacks into NASA and military computers. We know that he definitely did do this and that the U.S. government very badly wanted to extradite and charge him with these crimes. Did they want to be able to shut him up? Secondly, again, we have President Reagan's strange diary entry.

Additionally and oddly, this was around the same time that Reagan also initiated the Strategic Defense Initiative, the so-called "Star Wars" program. We also know billions were spent on this, but little if anything was made public about where all that black project money went, or what was accomplished with it. Then, we have the statements and claims by "Captain Kaye" and others who claimed to have been in the secret space fleet, as well Gary McKinnon's assertion he had seen documents testifying to the existence of such a fleet with even a list of officers.

Although there is no "smoking gun" most assuredly with regard to the idea of the Solar Warden space fleet, one does have to consider all this as pointing to the fact that something does seem to have been going on. This "something" has not been told to the public, which of course, makes us suspicious.

Again, where and how was all that black project money spent for the Star Wars program? How could we send so many more people into space in one go than NASA's shuttles could possibly hope to manage? Why is the U.S. government so intent on trying to extradite a young man who stole nothing from their computers and merely showed that they could be hacked into?

Was, or is there still a Solar Warden space fleet, one capable of easily sending ships to Mars and even land there and come back without problems, or perhaps even shoot down Earth probes sent there out of fear of discovery of this fact? Well, there is one other item we should not overlook in this regard, as well. This is the Orion Project.

The Orion Project, theorized and even with designs begun by the U.S. government back in the 1950's, was based on the idea that nuclear explosions near the base of a rocket could give such a vehicle enormous thrust and incredible speeds. As time went by, this design was refined with the idea of using small fusion or fission explosions, instead. The rocket would detonate the explosions, tiny nuclear bombs in a stream or series of "pulses" inside a shielded well at the ship's base (please see image below).

Modern Pulsed Fission Propulsion Concept, Orion
Source: Wikimedia, Public Domain

To be clear on this, such a concept is well within our current technological capabilities. Actually, it was even within our capabilities, or very close to being so, back in the 1950's. What seemed to put a stop to the idea (if, indeed, it was really stopped), was the problem of all that nuclear radiation in our atmosphere. The Atmospheric Test Ban Treaty, which the United States signed, effectively seemed to have stopped development of such a powerful but radiation-polluting rocket.

So why have I bothered to add this here? Well, for one thing, it is theorized that instead of taking 150 to 300 days, almost a year, an Orion rocket could make it to Mars in just about 30 days! Just 30 days! Imagine! Moreover, the carrying capacity of such a vehicle would be almost unlimited compared to today's rockets. In fact, it is even theorized a rocket the size of a small city could be sent to Alpha Centauri, our nearest neighboring star this way, complete with an entire colony on board the vessel and all the necessities it might need.

Make no mistake; this is no piece of fantasy science fiction! Again, even in the 1950's, we had the capability of building such a vehicle, and now with the advances in technology that have been made since then, almost some 70 years ago, we certainly could achieve such a goal with comparative ease.

The question is; have we developed the Orion rocket, but just in secret? Do these ships form a secret space fleet known as Solar Warden? If the government constructed such ships in space, how would we know if they even existed?

So have we a fleet of Orion-style spaceships? I will leave it to you to decide, but again, the idea is intriguing. If we have, then trips to Mars would be among the more mundane and quicker things we could accomplish and due to the dangers of cosmic rays, far safer because of the much shorter duration they would take.

One final note here; if we don't have a space fleet, or extraterrestrials don't, then what are all those "things" in NASA photographs hovering around our sun? What is it NASA is pixelating out of the images, and by the way, doing such a poor job of hiding the fact they are doing it, in the process? Again, I leave it to you to decide.

CHAPTER 18—Project Pegasus

Project Pegasus. As conspiracy theories go, this is most definitely one of the odder ones and yet, there are certain elements of it that have the ring of truth to them...to a point. Andrew Basiago, a Seattle lawyer, has declared that he was once in something known as Project Pegasus, a secret government project. From the age of seven to twelve, Andrew said that this U.S. black project's purpose was to achieve the ability to teleport, and seemingly (inadvertently?) to be able to travel through time, as well. This program was, according to Basiago, under the auspices of DARPA, or again, the Defense Advanced Reach Projects Agency.

In this program, Basiago also claimed that, as he put it:

"They trained children along with adults so they could test the mental and physical effects of time travel on kids. Also, children had an advantage over adults in terms of adapting to the strains of moving between past, present, and future."

Despite the incredible nature of his claim, another attorney, Alfred Webre, and a supposed expert in exopolitics, made the extraordinary statement that this capability of Project Pegasus had already been in use for close to 40 years, but the Department of Defense had kept it secret for understandable reasons of secrecy. They wished to avoid the Soviets and other enemy governments gaining such abilities.

It is one thing to teleport a subatomic particle and/or a simple atom, as has already been done, make no mistake about that, but to send something or someone through time or space that way would be at an incredible price one would think. However, the ability to teleport does not seem too difficult after all, at least not cost-wise, because Alfred Webre went on to state:

"It's an inexpensive, environmentally friendly means of transportation."

According to Andrew Basiago, the ability to time travel and teleport came about when the government seized Nikola Tesla's papers from his belongings at his apartment upon his demise in 1943. They then used this information, developed it, and created the teleportation/time travel device.

The apparatus sounds like something from a mad scientist's laboratory, and apparently, over time, eight different methods or systems of teleportation/time travel came about from Tesla's work as the project kept refining the technology. As Basiago put it:

"The machine consisted of two gray elliptical booms about eight feet tall, separated by about 10 feet, between which a shimmering curtain of what Tesla called 'radiant energy' was broadcast. Radiant energy is a form of energy that Tesla discovered that is latent and pervasive in the universe and has among its properties the capacity to bend time-space."

As with the *Star Gate* movie and television series, those who wished to travel through time or space simply had to pass through this curtain of Tesla's radiant energy. They would enter what he called a "vortal tunnel" (seemingly very reminiscent of the old TV series, *The Time Tunnel)*. And as he also put it:

"...when the tunnel closed, we found ourselves at our destination. One felt either as if one was moving at a great rate of speed or moving not at all, as the universe was wrapped around one's location."

Basiago also insists there is evidence of his having time traveled. For instance, he points to a photograph (please see below) of a boy standing in a cluster of people at Gettysburg, where Abraham Lincoln gave his famous speech in 1863. His translocation in time and space to Gettysburg was from a hidden lab in East Hanover, New Jersey. However, apparently, his trip didn't quite go as planned, because he said:

"I had been dressed in period clothing, as a Union bugle boy. I attracted so much attention at the Lincoln speech site at Gettysburg wearing oversized men's street shoes that I left the area around the dais and walked about 100 paces over to where I was photographed in the Josephine Cogg image of Lincoln at Gettysburg."

Supposed Image of Basiago with oversized adult shoes standing slightly apart from other boys in the foreground of the picture.
Source: Public Domain/Wikipedia

Andrew Basiago's claims don't stop there. He said that he also had time traveled to the night of Lincoln's assassination at the Ford Theatre, not just once, but on a number of occasions. He said:

"I did not, however, witness the assassination. Once, I was on the theater level when he was shot and I heard the shot followed by a great commotion that arose from the crowd. It was terrible to hear."

In an odd aside to all this, Basiago said that no two visits to the past were ever quite the same, but that it was:

"...like they were sending us to slightly different alternative realities on adjacent timelines. As these visits began to accumulate, I twice ran into myself during two different visits."

There were odd side effects of this repeated traveling to the same location in that he was there at the same time as other versions of himself supposedly were. As he also stated:

"After the first of these two encounters with myself occurred, I was concerned that my cover might be blown. Unlike the jump to Gettysburg, in which I was clutching a letter to Navy Secretary Gideon Welles to offer me aid and assistance in the event I was arrested, I didn't have any explanatory materials when I was sent to Ford's Theatre."

Of course, getting there was one thing, but getting back was another. Basiago also claimed that Project Pegasus used a "holographic" method to allow him and others to return to the present. This permitted them not only to transport physically through time, but they could do it in a virtual manner, as well. Basiago stated:

"If we were in the hologram for 15 minutes or fewer, the hologram would collapse, and after about 60 seconds of standing in a field of supercharged particles, we would find ourselves back on the stage in the present."

Project Pegasus was not without its problem or fatalities, it seems. Adults had a much harder time traveling than children seemed to and it was theorized this was because that by adulthood, most people's minds had become too set, too hardwired to our current reality to deal with such spacetime translocations. Basiago says that passage through the vortal could be very rough. In addition, Alfred Webre even claimed that one child suffered horribly this way, unable to transport all at one time. He claims the child, upon completion of the transfer had his upper body appear in the new time/location before his legs did, thus effectively having amputated them in the process. As he put it:

"He was writhing in pain with just stumps where his legs had been."

However, Webre also went on to say such terrible side effects had since been resolved. Basiago also stated that although there were a fair number of people involved in this project, the total was probably only around 100 people participating in it at any time.

How does this involve Mars? Well, Basiago also claimed that while in Project Pegasus, he also teleported to the red planet. He stated in a white paper of 2008 that:

There is life on Mars. Evidence that the red planet harbors life and has for eons was discovered by the author by examining NASA photograph PIA 10214, a westward view of the West Valley of the Columbia Basin in the Gusev Crater that was taken by the Mars Exploration Rover Spirit in November 2007 and beamed back to the Earth.

Chapter Conclusion: As incredible as Andrew Basiago and Alfred Webre's claims seem to be, it is odd that both men, who are attorneys would risk their livelihoods, and certainly their careers on making such outlandish claims. One has to wonder why someone would threaten their own incomes to such a remarkable degree to make such fantastic claims. Money would hardly seem the answer. Yes, for a year or two they might be able to achieve some good income from such a false claim or hoax, as in writing a book, the lecture circuit, etc., but this could hardly compare, long-term, to what they could make as practicing attorneys (unless, of course, they were terrible at that, which seems unlikely).

Furthermore, there is no doubt that doing such a thing would subject them to incredible ridicule and abuse of various sorts. This is not something anyone would entertain doing lightly. Therefore, if this is a hoax, it seems a rather pointless one.

Finally, both men passed the bar to become attorneys. Anyone who knows anything about what it takes to become a lawyer knows that it is a long and arduous process, and takes a very good I.Q. to accomplish. Again, why would they risk all their long-term chievements in this regard to create such a hoax or lie? Surely, it would not further their careers in law to do so, but instead would make them a laughing stock amongst those others, their peers in their profession.

Was Project Pegasus real, or is this just another hoax or crazy conspiracy theory? Again, when one lacks any firmer proof in such matters, one can only conjecture. Therefore, once more, I leave it to the reader to decide for themselves as to the veracity (or not) of this particular conspiracy theory. However, if true, it lends credence to the idea that people, and/or other beings have been on Mars, and apparently recently.

CHAPTER 19—Ancient Aliens From Mars?

Ancient Alien conspiracy theorists have long held the view that aliens have walked this planet, perhaps even now, but certainly in our remote past, as well. Two main sources for their arguments, although they have many, and some appear quite credible, include the discoveries made at the ruins of the cities of Harappa and Mohenjo-Daro, as discussed earlier in this book.

No one can account for the areas of higher background radiation at these sites, so high, in fact, that again, they closed Mohenjo-Daro to the public for just this reason. That means dangerous levels of radiation! What with radioactive skeletons and such, the site was considered just to unsafe for prolonged exposure by either archaeologists or the public. So how did this come about?

Well, the writings of the Vedic texts, particularly the Mahabharata and the Ramayana have their own ancient version of just how this happened. These texts give extensive and detailed accounts of "god" overlords of humans and a great war that took place on Earth and in space, again as mentioned earlier in this book.

Another source, as also earlier mentioned, are the cuneiform, clay-tablet writings of the ancient Sumerians. They speak of the Anunnaki, a race of beings "sent from heaven to Earth." Austen Layard unearthed clay tablets, which spoke of the Anunnaki when he explored the ruins of Nineveh, an ancient city, and one mentioned in the Bible. Among his discoveries were "The Seven Tablets of Creation." These spoke of the Anunnaki descending to Earth and creating us humans.

Another researcher of some repute, Zecharia Sitchin, also translated the cuneiform tablets. His conclusion was that the Anunnaki created humans as their slaves, to wait on them in their temples/palaces, and to do mining for them, since they, themselves, were ill suited for such tasks on Earth, not being originally from this planet.

Based directly on the information from his work, many Ancient Astronaut proponents claim that either the Anunnaki came to our solar system from another one with a planet named Nibiru, or alternatively, this planet was far out on the edge of our own solar system. The Anunnaki then colonized our system; at least, they did with regard to Mars and the Earth.

Ancient Alien theorists also show the ancient Sumerians' large number of so-called myths about the red planet to bolster this idea and claim there wouldn't be such a high number of tales about that world unless there was some truth of sorts to them. They point out, for instance, that Venus does not hold nearly such a privileged position in Sumerian legends, although it has a much brighter presence in the night sky than Mars, which makes such a thing odd in itself. One would think the brightest objects in the sky would have the tales created about them, and not the not-so-bright ones.

The theory goes that the Anunnaki used Mars as a sort of stopover, or outpost on their trips to and from Earth, or perhaps had minimally colonized it, as well. Again, researchers point to the numerous anomalies on Mars of what appear to be statues, ruins, tracks, roads, and even skeletons as evidence for the presence of the ancient Anunnaki, of their having colonized that planet.

However, if one is to believe the ancient texts of the Sumerian tablets, they tell a history of Mars that is incredible. They claim some catastrophic happening demolished not only the Anunnaki colony(ies) on Mars, but also did much to wreak havoc on the planet itself.

Oddly, there is a form of corroboration for this tale from the other side of the world, in Central America and the north of South America, as well. Here, "myths" tell of a giant feathered serpent that attacked Mars and destroyed everything on it. Of course, a feathered serpent might be those ancient people's way of described a comet, perhaps? Or maybe, it was a plasma strike?

Elongated skulls. There is one final oddity about this, as well. For decades now, Ancient Alien theorists have pointed to the discovery in various locations around the world of elongated skulls. They have been found as far apart as Peru and Egypt, for example, and even in Asia.

At first, these were dismissed by archaeologists as just those people deliberately deforming the heads of their children to grow with these types of shaped skulls for some weird aesthetic reason or other. Yes, some Ancient Alien theorists say they did this to emulate their overlords or masters, the Anunnaki. People often imitate those they think are superior to themselves. Moreover, yes, there is evidence that many of these skulls were deliberately malformed by strapping boards to the child's head, forcing the skull to grow in an elongated fashion.

Just who or what these ancients were trying to emulate by forcing their children to grow up with elongated skulls is a matter for some fierce debate. However, other elongated skulls have been found, as well, and they do not seem to be a product of such deliberate malformations. How do we know this? Because:

1. These other elongated skulls have a greater cranial capacity than the deliberately malformed skulls do. Change the shape of a child's skull all you want, alter it to elongate if you like, but that child's overall cranial capacity is not altered. There isn't any difference in the cranial capacity of a child, or later adult, with a deliberately elongated skull from any other humans.

However, the other elongated skulls that were found do have a markedly greater cranial capacity.

2. Unlike the deliberately malformed skulls, which have the natural "suture" marks where the skull knits together as the child matures, these other skulls do not have the same types of suture markings.

3. Tests have shown that the purposely malformed skulls (elongated) still have the same bone structure as the rest of us. However, the other skulls do not. The bone material is "fibrous," in nature, as one scientist put it.

Are these then the skulls of human/alien hybrids, or even of the ancient Anunnaki overlords themselves? If so, some anomalies on Mars look very similar to these elongated skulls and if that is what they truly are, then we have an ancient race on Mars and one on Earth with the same types of heads. (Please see photo below.)

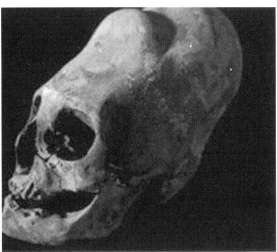

Elongated skull found on Earth
Source: Public Domain

An elongated skull on Mars or just an odd rock?
Source: NASA

Is the above picture a skull on Mars from ancient aliens or hybrids, or again, just an odd rock? Well, we know the ones on Earth are in two distinct groups with the "odd" ones having different suture marks, and a different makeup of the bone material. Moreover, when the Director of the Paracas History Museum sent samples for analysis, it was found that some of the DNA from the skulls was "unknown" or "not human."

So if the Anunnaki did colonize Mars, and then later died there, or were forced to retreat from the planet, and in the process witnessed the destruction of the biosphere of Mars, just how did it happen?

Well, again, we have Dr. John Brandeburg who claims an ancient civilization on Mars was wiped out by a nuclear attack from another alien race. Again, he believes there might have been two races on Mars, the "Cydonians," as well as the "Utopians." He states that it is his theory both races were obliterated in what amounted to genocide.

Once more, he cites the evidence for such an event by the fact that:

"The Martian surface is covered with a thin layer of radioactive substances including uranium, thorium and radioactive potassium - and this pattern radiates from a hot spot on Mars…. A nuclear explosion could have sent debris all around the planet."

Remember, these isotopes are the same as those we ourselves have observed here on Earth from atmospheric nuclear bomb tests. Therefore, it is reasonable to conclude that such a thing might have happened on Mars, as well, or how else did these isotopes get there? We have no other easy answer other than to say a "naturally occurring" explosion from a georeactor must have taken place, and yet, there is little evidence for that, if any. As for there being two alien races, was one the Anunnaki, and the other one us, their forced servants/slaves? They could have taken us there, as well.

Chapter Conclusion: Again, there is no "smoking gun" form of evidence with regard to ancient aliens being on Earth and Mars. However, there does seem to be a good deal of supportive information from different sources, e.g., the Vedic Texts of India, the Mesoamerican stories, etc., to suggest that perhaps aliens were not only here on Earth in our distant past, but might just have been on Mars, too. Besides this, we have Dr. Brandburg's contention that there was a civilization on Mars in ancient times, and that it died in a nuclear holocaust.

So were there ancient aliens on Mars? Well, evidence for them seems to be building in the forms of photos of what appear to be ruins, statues, pyramids, etc., as well as for objects, such as a UFO flying through the Martian skies, and radioactive isotopes.

214

Added to this, we have worldwide legends of a race of beings who visited Earth, and apparently visited Mars. These same legends and texts speak of a great war; one that the stories say exacted great devastation on the red planet. Coincidence only—or is there something to all of this? Again, the reader must decide for himself.

Still, there is even more evidence regarding this idea. In the next chapter, we will discuss this other evidence.

CHAPTER 20—Remote Viewers See Mars?

In line with all the conspiracy theories is a particularly strange one, and yet it does in many instances have the ring of truth about and even CIA documents to back it up. Remote viewing, or the ability of someone to be given a set of coordinates as a target, and nothing more, and being able to somehow telepathically see the area and draw, as well as describe it, is something that our government, through the auspices of the CIA, actually tried to do. There were some very interesting results!

The CIA tested a number of remote viewers. This was at the height of the Cold War with the (then) Soviet Union (now the Russian Federation). Spying on each other was something that was common then and still is now, and government agencies went to some extreme lengths to try to do this at the time.

Among the remote viewers was a man by the name of Ingo Swann. Now, this man claimed even before documents were released under the Freedom of Information Act that he had taken part in such remote viewing tests back in the 1970's. It seems, judging by the documentation more recently released that he actually did. Otherwise, how would he have known about the program before the government divulged that it existed?

Ostensibly, his story as a remote viewer began around early 1973. Ingo Swann, a professed psychic became involved with the CIA at that point. This was in an experiment that involved him trying remotely to view Jupiter. This much seems to be true because the official records of the experiment, which involved not only the CIA, but the NSA, and even Stanford University, as well, all sate this.

The session started. Ingo Swann felt himself "viewing" the planet Jupiter. One of the things he noticed was that Jupiter had a ring around it, not nearly as impressive as the rings around Saturn, but a definite ring, even so. This information was astounding because later and well after the time of this experiment, the Pioneer 10 verified from its photos that there was, indeed, a ring around the giant planet. Up until this time, the ring had been unknown. Therefore, the photos from the Pioneer 10 seemed to verify Swann's accuracy in this matter of remote viewing.

Later, in 1975, a man who went by the pseudonym of Axelrod approached him. He told Swann that he again would contact him with regard to the possibility of a special and very secret project. A few weeks later, this occurred. Mr. Axelrod, in their next meeting instructed Swann to go to the National Museum of Natural History. There, Axelrod met with Swann and then via various means of transportation, took him (blindfolded at one point) to a secret place. Swann, judging by what little sensory input he got while being thus blindfolded, had the impression he had been taken to an underground military base, but he couldn't be sure.

After asking Swann questions about his psychic capabilities, he was told he would be extremely well paid if he applied his services to the benefit of the United States government, but that his work was extremely sensitive and very top secret. The next thing Axelrod did was have Swann use some coordinates to remote view a site on the Moon. Swann, after some effort, found himself viewing the Moon as if he were there, but it was the far side he was seeing, and he said he could view a number of buildings, some dome-shaped, some not.

As he accustomed himself to this incredible experience, Swann realized there were beings of some sort occupying the structures. In addition, spookily enough, Swann said it was as if those beings could sense his presence, which frightened him some. He ended that session of remote viewing at this point. When Swann mentioned that the beings he saw didn't seem to be human, Axelrod purportedly said:

"Isn't that something, huh?"

So impressive were the results of the remote viewer program that yet another project was funded shortly after this one ended. Project Stargate, as it was called, was launched in 1978.

How does this relate to Mars as a conspiracy theory and/or something that really occurred regarding that planet? Well, in 1984, the CIA then focused their attention on Mars and asked their remote viewers to attempt to "see" the planet, given a specific set of coordinates for it. It is important to note here that the participant remote viewers were not told it was Mars, but were just given a set of coordinates, which to their knowledge should have been some place on Earth.

Now, according to one of the documents attained under the Freedom of Information Act, a now declassified one, the viewer gave an incredible response. Remember, he did not know that the coordinates were for Mars, or anywhere else in space, but just Earth, presumably.

What did he see? Well, he "saw" a place on Mars that had pyramids. He also saw what to him were very advanced examples of technology, as well as "seeing" creatures that looked like tall versions of us humans. They appeared to be on the brink of some sort of calamity, probably to do with their climate, environment, or biosphere. Even more intriguing is what he saw in the famous/infamous region of Mars known as Cydonia. This is where photos do show "pyramid-like" objects, as well as the mysterious image of the Martian "face." Some claim there are also ruins of a city near this site. Moreover, these were the very coordinates given him!

Pyramids on Mars, not far from the "face."
Source: NASA, 1976.

Please understand. The CIA was very intent on this project of Remote Viewing. They tested it repeatedly, spent a great deal of funds on it, and were actually pleased with the accuracy of the results from the project. They concluded remote viewing was a tool that could help America in its efforts to spy on its foes. As stated in this document:

SECRET

IAGPA-F-SD   09 May 1984

MEMORANDUM FOR RECORD

SUBJECT: Security Review of "MIND WARS" (U)

1. (U) Reference; MIND WARS; The True Story of Secret
Government Research into the Military Potential of Psychic
Weapons; by Ron McRae; St. Martin's Press, New York; 1984.

2. (S/CL-1/NOFORN) There are twenty three (23) specific
references to Remote Viewing, its use, or accuracy made in
statements by; Barbara Honegger, Hal Puthof, Russel Targ, LTC
John Alexander, Congressman Rose, Ingo Swann, G. Gordon Liddy,
and two additional but unnamed individuals purportedly working
in the area of psychoenergetics with the CIA (See attached
inclosure).

3. (S/CL-1/NOFORN) In reviewing the book the following
statements can be determined as having a high reliability for
truth:

    a. Remote Viewing (RV) is real, it is accurate, is
replicable, is being pursued by at least the CIA, Navy, Army and
Pentagon in general. That it is being pursued for intelligence
and military applications.

    b. The government's interest in RV is clearly
"applications" oriented.

    c. Stanford Research Institute International (SRI-I) is the
key institute involved with the government in RV research and
Development. The specific individual is Dr. Hal Puthoff.

            WARNING NOTICE: CENTER LANE SPECIAL ACCESS PROGRAM
        RESTRICT DISSEMINATION TO THOSE WITH VERIFIED ACCESS
                    TO CATEGORY TWO (2)

        SENSITIVE INTELLIGENCE SOURCES AND METHODS INVOLVED

            NOT RELEASABLE TO FOREIGN NATIONALS

                        CLASSIFIED BY: CDR, INSCOM
                        DECLASSIFY ON: OADR

Source: Public Domain

Notice Paragraph Number 3, where it says:

"In reviewing...(a) Remote Viewing (RV) is real, it is accurate, is replicable, is being pursued by at least the CIA, Navy, Army and Pentagon in general. That it is being pursued for intelligence and military applications."

By the way, what Ingo Swann saw on Mars was in ancient times, not now. The controller of the experiment, Mr. Axelrod, had then asked Swann to move forward in time to the present day and to view the planet that way. Swann complied and stated that the planet's civilization was in ruins that seemed very old. Moreover, this means remote viewers aren't just limited to the past and present, but can even see the future, as well, it would seem.

As strange as remote viewing may sound to us, it could well be based on real science. The minds of these remote viewers may seem to be able to have the "nonlocal" nature or ability instantly to move around in space or time, even as the "spooky action at a distance," as Albert Einstein described it, works on the quantum level for paired particles.

Additionally, recent study results, repeated often now, have shown the human consciousness seems to exist partly in the future, as well as in the present. In fact, the human mind apparently can "see" the future anywhere from two to ten seconds ahead of time based on those studies. Yes, they are real studies done at impeccable institutions with real results and one can check them for one's self.

These studies, performed and repeated at various universities and research centers have shown through experiments that humans can and do react to random photographs of horrible sights two to ten seconds before they see them.

The "horrible" photographs are placed randomly into a series of "nice" photographs of pleasant things and even the researchers themselves are unaware of when they will appear. This is to maintain strict control of the experiment. The results show that the subjects of the experiment (over and over) reacted to the negative photos shortly before they appeared on screen, but the length of time involved varied from individual to individual.

Therefore, the fact the human mind may not be subject to time as we see it, might imply that not only can some humans "see" things in the past or future, but also that the human mind, again, might be "nonlocal" in nature when it comes to space/time. That is, it is not subject to the laws of physics as we now understand them, but seems to be governed more by quantum physics, instead.

Chapter Conclusion: In this chapter, we have discussed remote viewing and the results obtained from it. Nonetheless, is this idea of remote viewing all nonsense, or is there something to it? Well, we know this much:

1. There were at least two remote viewing programs with a number of participants who had varying degrees of accuracy in their results. Some volunteers were spot on in their viewing, others were only partly accurate, and others still achieved no real concrete results at all.

2. Ingo Swann was considered a highly accurate remote viewer and his accuracy was confirmed by "seeing" the ring around Jupiter before scientists here on Earth even knew it existed. He also seems to have confirmed the fact that there is something or someone on the far side of the Moon. So it is reasonably to conclude he is just as accurate, at least, about Mars.

3. The CIA was so impressed with the results that they recommended the project be not only continued, but also used as an information gathering source and/or for committing espionage against America's enemies. The document included above clearly states much of this.

Therefore, we can conclude that remote viewing seems to work and often works well, at least in the estimation of the CIA. By simple deduction, then Ingo Swann's viewings, proven correct on other matters, could well be correct about Mars. Once there was intelligent life there, even as legends, Sumerian cuneiform writings, and the Vedic Texts of India here on Earth declared there was, and that the civilization died in a calamity of some sort.

This, too, may not be a "smoking gun" piece of evidence, but it is getting very close to that, even so. This is something definitely to consider as we move on. Combined with other evidence discussed in other chapters, the cumulative weight of all this is getting to be compelling.

CHAPTER 21—Rh Negative Humans The Remaining Aliens?

This conspiracy theory is a truly strange one, but again, seems to have some basis in fact. Among human beings, there are different blood types. These are A, B, AB, and O. These are referred to as "positive" if they test positive for a certain antigen (or proteins found on the surface of cells) that are also found in the Rhesus Monkey, among others primates. Those who don't have this are referred to as "negative" because they lack the antigen. Worldwide, only about seven percent of the human race has the Rh Negative factor. In the United States, that number is a bit higher, being almost 15 percent of the American population.

The Rh Negative factor seems to have first appeared in central Europe, and estimates vary, but some say as recently as just 3,500 years ago. Despite this, some populations don't have the RH Negative factor at all, since the dispersal of this factor takes time, as populations intermingle and have offspring that might have it.

Weirdly, the Rh Negative factor is a big problem for scientists. If it is a natural mutation of some sort, as they think it might be, it is a bad one in some respects. Rh Negative mothers can have many problems in pregnancies if their unborn child happens to be positive or vice versa. In the past, before modern medicine, both mother and baby frequently died in childbirth. Today, with our medical technology, this isn't nearly such a problem, but even so, mothers who are Rh Negative must seek a doctor's help to insure their pregnancies go well.

This means that Rh Negative people, in a sense, are almost a different species of sort. The definition of a species is if it can't interbreed with other like-kind species, and so it is separate and considered distinct. Although Rh-Negative and Rh-Positive people can still breed, it is only with much difficulty, and as mentioned above, often resulted in the deaths of both mother and child. The mortality rate used to be very high.

Furthermore, scientists are at a loss as to why people still have the Rh-Negative factor at all. Positive people, being so at odds with Rh-Negative people, and so having it so often culminated in the deaths when interbreeding between the two groups took place, that researchers can't figure out why Rh-Negative people simply weren't weeded out of the population by now, as happens with many lethal mutations. Slowly but surely, Rh-Negative people should have dwindled in numbers, being such a small group to start with, and over the millennia dying so often in childbirth. Yet, this doesn't seemed to have happened. If anything, the reverse seems true, and this again goes contrary to what we think we know about evolution and naturally occurring mutations, especially ones that can be lethal to the host under certain conditions.

How did this all come about? Well, for that we have to backtrack a little...

With the deciphering of the human genome, a rather dismaying discovery was made. Scientists had long thought that humans possessed far more genes than other animals, even the other primates, and this accounted for us being so different in some ways from them. This did not turn out to be the case.

The human genome contains only around 19,000 to 20,000 genes, not the expected 140,000 or even 100,000 (later revised down to this last number). This came as a shock to scientists that we weren't even double that of the genome of the common fruit fly! To make matters worse, the vast majority of genes were the same as those of other animals. They are almost 99 percent the same as the chimpanzee, for example.

Worse, many of our genes were not just the same as those of other animals, but even as those of many plants!

However, there was one important result. It did show that all life on Earth uses the same DNA, if not all having the same genes or same number of them. Still, there was one thing that struck researchers as very odd. There were some genes, a little over 200 of them that did seem different from other life forms on Earth. They had no predecessors found in any other type of life on Earth.

Scientists can only account for these genes by saying they were acquired "horizontally." That is, they were not part of the evolutionary tree of life as science has envisioned it, and so not handed down to us from other, prior existing species in any way. Instead, they seem to have come to humans "laterally" or "sideways" (horizontally), instead. This is a discovery that has left many researchers scratching their heads and wondering just how this could have happened.

Many researchers decided that perhaps we acquired these genes much more recently in our species' history, perhaps through infection by bacteria that carried them or even caused mutations in existing genes somehow. Yet, to acquire so many so late on in our evolution goes contrary to what we thought we knew about how long it takes for this sort of thing to take place. It is supposed to be a slow and gradual process.

Some argue these genes and the Rh Negative factor have been added by "something" or "someone." In other words, "something" must have interfered with our development as a species. They think we were genetically tinkered with on purpose and this has made us different from the other ape species on our planet.

Added to this is the specifically weird problem of Rh Negative people. By the way, the difference between those and Rh Positive people seems to go even further than just blood types. Often, Rh Negative persons seem to have a marked creative bent. Many, much more than probability would indicate, have a higher than average I.Q. They also are often left-handed, though not all, and even their eyes and hair coloring seem to follow certain "types."

Moreover, some researchers even claim that Rh-Negative people are "watched" by our government, since they might have a marked disposition toward certain psychic abilities, especially remote viewing (as mentioned in the previous chapter). Some even say Rh-Negative people who show signs of such abilities (while being surveilled), are recruited into the government psychic programs, such as remote viewing.

Some conspiracy theorists go even further. They suggest the government will make such people disappear if they do not agree to be recruited. This is out of fear an enemy government might find and use them for their own purposes, instead.

The Anunnaki and genetics. Now we come to that other conspiracy theory that says the Anunnaki, that ancient race of godlike beings who the ancient Sumerians believed ruled the Earth, and their possible involvement in all this. Remember, Anunnaki is the Sumerian name for "Those who from heaven to Earth came." According to the Sumerian texts and Ancient Alien theorists, it seemed that the Anunnaki originally came to Earth seeking gold.

Gold as it turns out, is probably rare throughout the universe, because even supernovas and hypernovas don't produce gold when they explode. It takes something more, and cosmologists and astronomers think it has to be approximately something like two neutron stars colliding to produce gold as a byproduct of such titanic collisions, a rare event. It seems gold is rare everywhere and that's why the Anunnaki came to Earth to mine it.

They had a problem. According to the texts, the Anunnaki were ill suited to our environment. From the descriptions, it would seem this was a real hurdle for them. The solution they came up with was genetically to modify one of the existing species on Earth (us), to enhance them, so they could better understand and perform tasks for the Anunnaki. Of course and even as the Bible intimates with the "Fallen" or the "Watchers,"or "Nephilim," the new species would have to be similar to themselves in some respects, if only so they could work better for their new masters. The Bible even claims there was interbreeding between the so-called Fallen/Watchers, and humans.

Again, humans, according to the cuneiform writings of the ancient Sumerians, were the result of this genetic tinkering. Some even say there is evidence for this in our history in the form of leftover symbols. They point, for example, to the staff of medicine, entwined with two serpents forming a double helix. As most of us now know, the DNA molecule is a double helix, so Ancient Alien theorists believe this is a "leftover" symbol of the Anunnaki reign here on Earth, and their medical control of us indigenous humans.

Part of this genetic tinkering of us included introducing the Anunnaki's own Rh Negative factor to us, so that we would be more compatible with their genetic engineering (using their genes?). This means, the theorists argue, that the unaccounted for genes in the human genome, and the Rh Negative factor were the result of aliens having modified us to better suit their needs.

If you think this is a minor thing, being Rh Negative, just go online sometime and run a search on the subject. YouTube and practically every other major forum on the Internet speak about this issue, with numerous groups (some open and some closed) dealing with the topic of being Rh Negative. Some even claim that Rh Negative people are evil, descendants of aliens, and now control our planet. They point to the large number of Rh Negative people in positions of power, such as the royal family of Great Britain that has many Rh Negative members in it. Therefore, conspiracy theories on this subject are rife.

The point here is that many think a branch of humans are technically, alien-human hybrids and they point to some being Rh Negative as a sign of this, since it seems to so go against normal evolutionary theory in this regard, that it even still exists, or ever came to exist in the first place. Over 99 percent of all naturally occurring mutations are lethal for those members of a species who have this happen to them, so they don't live to breed. So why this mutation, Rh Negative, continues in a small but measureable portion of the human population is unexplained.

If you think all this is just stuff and nonsense, that there isn't anything to the whole idea of Rh Negative people being part alien, you might have to think again. It would seem such people might often strive for positions of power. For example, every president of the United States since (and including) Dwight D. Eisenhower, meaning for the last 70 years, approximately, has been Rh Negative! That's right, all of them, including supposedly, even Barak Obama and Donald Trump, based on the sources I searched. This is so, as far as the researchers involved tell us.

Ask yourself this: if Rh Negative people are only 15 percent of the American population (again, just seven percent worldwide), what are the odds that every president for the better part of the last century (and perhaps before, but we don't have blood type records going back that far...), should be Rh Negative? For a few presidents to be Rh Negative would just be a matter of favorable probabilities happening, despite their low incidence in the general human population. But for all of them to be that way? Again, just something to think about, since this happening really does seem to fly in the face of what we know about genetics, and about the laws of probability.

Chapter Conclusion. The fact that a small percentage of the human population is Rh Negative is a given. It is not a matter for debate or discussion. The fact it seems an entirely negative and often lethal mutation means it should have been swiftly weeded out of the human genome is also not in question. Dead people don't breed and those that die while trying to achieve the same result also are weeded out; the mutated gene is bred out of the human population, or should be, theoretically. It is also a fact that this does not seem to be the case in this particular instance.

What does this mean? If Rh Negative people should long ago have disappeared from the human population, then what accounts for them still being here? Moreover, what are those 200-plus genes in the human genome that researchers can't account for as having been handed down to us by past species on our evolutionary tree?

For many conspiracy theorists, this means that some (or even all) of humanity have some degree of "alien" heritage in them. By simple logic, if this is so, this means there were ancient aliens here on Earth who intervened in our genetic code. In addition, from this we can deduce that quite likely, aliens or the Anunnaki as the Sumerians called them, were here. If they were here, then they could well have been on Mars, as well. Moreover, by further extension of this logic, all the ancient texts and legends that speak of the destruction of Mars and the Anunnaki or whatever alien race they were, could well be true.

An interesting side note is that perhaps humans are the alien race? In our next chapter, we will discuss this.

CHAPTER 22—Are Humans Actually Aliens?

Now we come to another question; what if we are the aliens? What if we are the Martians? This is yet another conspiracy theory, but one which does seem to have some valid points to it. Nevertheless, exactly how is it that we could be the aliens on what we think of as our own planet, one where we evolved? Well, there are a number of conspiracy theories in this regard, but I'll give the main ones here.

First, there is an American doctor, an ecologist, Dr. Ellis Silver who makes a strong case for the idea humans, modern humans that is, are not from this Earth. In his book, *Humans are not from Earth: a scientific evaluation of the evidence,* he points to the huge number of ailments we suffer as a species here on this planet and makes the powerful argument that other animal species here do not suffer from nearly so many of those ills.

In his new book, a highly controversial one, Dr. Silver states flat out that he doesn't believe humans are from Earth. He believes we were put here millennia ago, perhaps even tens of thousands of years ago. He even went so far as to suggest that Earth might be a place of exile, or what amounts to a prison planet.

This is a chilling thought in its own right and even more so, if one buys into the theory there are aliens on our Moon, on its far side, as many believe, and as there seems to be a great deal of evidence for. Would that make them our prison wardens, if so? Again, a chilling thought….

Dr. Silver centers this idea on the fact humans seem to be an incredibly violent species, especially amongst ourselves. Of all the animals on the planet, none is so capable of killing members of its own species in the thousands and millions as we are, and often we've done just that. For example, the number of dead in each of the last century's two great world wars numbered in the millions. Dr. Silver hypothesizes that perhaps we have been placed under a sort of quarantine, and must stay within our solar system and not fraternize with any other alien races until we've learned to better control our baser natures.

Yes, this is all just conjecture on his part and could easily be dismissed as such if it weren't for an array of facts he summons in his book to make a case for his point of view. For instance, he claims that humans show they are not from Earth because of all the physiological problems they have here, whereas many other animals on Earth do not. For example:

1. Humans have a constant and major problem with back issues. Who hasn't heard of someone, a friend, relative, or coworker for example, who hasn't had back problems? We are subject to this ill far more than any other vertebrate on the planet it seems to be. Men, women, and even some children all can suffer terribly from back problems, with many undergoing surgery and medications to help ease the problem. For many others, there seems no relief at all. Dr. Silver says other species on Earth do not have this issue.

He believes the reason we have all these back and neck problems is that we originally came from a planet with a lighter gravity. Our bodies, according to him, simply have not evolved to handle the heavier gravity of Earth, and so back pain and other back problems are the consequence of this, not to mention sundry other ills, which we also have that animals don't seem to.

2. Humans sunburn easily. In fact, we do. Just minutes for some, out in the sun, can result in a painful sunburn. Over the years, these can then lead to skin cancers and death, and often do. Other animals, largely, and according to Dr. Silver, don't have this problem, or if they do, not nearly to the same degree.

Dr. Silver hypothesizes that perhaps humans evolved on a world with a weaker, more distant, or smaller sun, one where the sunlight wasn't nearly so prone to burn us, because it wasn't as strong for whatever reason.

3. Dr. Silver also refers to the fact that childbirth throughout history for humans has been not only an extremely painful proposition for women, but also a deadly one. Until modern medicine changed things, death of the infant and/or the mother during childbirth was worse than common! In some regions, it still is bad.

4. Many humans strongly dislike many available foods here on Earth. He suggests this might be because these were not the food sources we originally evolved along with, and so they are alien and unpleasant to us humans.

5. Dr. Silver also states that he finds it very strange that babies are born with such large heads, which makes for difficult birthing, as well, and can result in the death of the mother in the process. He points to the fact that other animals do not suffer this problem to any real degree. It seems it's only us.

6. He also declares that Earth is probably not our planet, because we are not attuned to its 24–hour cycle as other species on Earth. Dr. Silver is convinced that one of the reasons humans have so many illnesses is because our internal clocks are biologically (evolutionary) out of synch with Earth's day. He points to studies that show people have better health if they allow their internal clocks to be synchronized with a 25-hour day, rather than Earth's 24 one. He states that sleep researchers have proven this true.

Moreover and again with regard to his claims in his book, *Humans Are Not From Earth: A Scientific Evaluation Of The Evidence,* he has said:

"Mankind is supposedly the most highly developed species on the planet, yet is surprisingly unsuited and ill-equipped for Earth's environment: harmed by sunlight, a strong dislike for naturally occurring foods, ridiculously high rates of chronic disease, and more."

He also says:

"This is not a modern condition; the same factors can be traced all the way back through mankind's history on Earth."

Dr. Silver means we humans never fit in well on this planet and in many different ways. Moreover, he comes to the same startling conclusion that many Ancient Alien theorists have. That is, he thinks that the "native" species of Earth, the Neanderthals perhaps, were hybridized with another species. He thinks this other species may not have been that far away from our solar system; maybe as close as the star system of Alpha Centauri, our nearest neighboring star system.

There is one other thing; he points to the fact that there is a real undercurrent among some of us that we just don't belong here on Planet Earth, that this isn't our "home." Many feel that this place "isn't it."

It is the contention of Dr. Silver that humans, as we are today, arrived on this planet sometime around 60,000 years ago, but perhaps as much as 200,000 years.

Mars our home world? If one takes what Dr. Silver proposes at face value, at least to some extent, then humans have to have come from a world that is smaller or at least has a lighter gravity, substantially so. Mars does. Its gravity is just 0.376 of Earth's gravity, so a person on Mars would weigh just about 38% of what they do here on Earth. This would mean far less in the way of back or neck problems for humans if they lived there.

Furthermore, Mars, being considerably further from the sun, being 141.6 million miles (remember, Earth is just about 93 million miles), the sun would be much weaker and so its ability to sunburn humans would be considerably less. This is, of course, if Mars had a protective atmosphere comparable to Earth's, which it no longer has, but is said to have had in the past.

There is another point in the favor of Mars having been humans' original home. That is the length of day on Mars. Again, on Earth, a day is about 24 hours long (23 hours, 56 minutes, 4.1 seconds in length). On Mars, a day is almost 25 hours long (24 hours, 37 minutes, 22 seconds), which puts it much closer to the human ideal day length of 25 hours than an Earth day.

In other words, we humans have an internal biological clock, a circadian rhythm more attuned to Mars time than to our own planet's! This is rather a compelling idea, is it not?

Of course, Mars as it is now could not support human life without protective equipment, suits, buildings, oxygen, etc. However, the hypothesis is that Mars might have once have been a more comfortable or a more "natural" home for humanity.

A war? Well, we've discussed other ideas about this; for instance, there is the theory that researchers proposed, of a large asteroid impact that caused the planet to partially be destroyed, as well as blasting off much of its atmosphere, and causing its protective magnetic field to collapse. The question that remains with this theory is when did this exactly happen? The event itself would have been quick, very quick. The major and initial consequences would have been quick as well, being just hours or days in length, perhaps.

So when did this occur? Was it millions of years ago, or just a few tens of millennia ago? Without more data, that evidence simply isn't available yet, but scientists believe it had to have been millions of years ago, or even more.

Ancient Alien theorists believe differently. They think that not only could such an event have occurred much more recently, with some saying even just 13,000 or 20,000 years ago, but that it might not have occurred at all. As mentioned earlier, there is the theory Mars had a nuclear war, which could have caused the same results.

What does this mean for humans on Mars? Well, if Mars was our original home, it was devastated one way or the other and so no longer became habitable. Whether or not there was a war, whether or not "we" won it, Mars still became a rapidly dying world. We had to go somewhere else. We either went as the few surviving winners of the war, or as a ragtag group of defeated refugees.

After arriving on Earth, faced with survival under horribly primitive conditions, we went through a long period where we lived the most basic lives of survival. This went on for generations. Racial amnesia set in. When finally we did begin to climb to our feet again, all memory of the cataclysm that brought us here was lost to racial memory, except in the form of myths and legends.

Chapter Conclusion: Are humans from another world originally? Dr. Silver thinks so and he marshals some persuasive evidence to support his theory. Back problems for human are common. Childbirth is dangerous, or at least was before we developed modern medical methods to handle the various problems, and yet women still die in childbirth at times. Sleep studies do show we function better when attuned to a 25-hour day (a Mars day?). In addition, yes, we do sunburn very easily compared to practically any other land-based species on the planet.

Is Dr. Silver right? Well, the jury is still out on that, but again, his evidence is intriguing, and in some cases, even compelling. As to whether or not we originated on Mars, as some people theorize, is still unknown of course, but again, they do offer some persuasive evidence that Mars at one time when it had a thicker atmosphere, might well have been a "better" place for humans. Mars just might have been our "real" home.

The truth is that now we simply can't say one way or the other. However, do ask yourself these questions: "Do you feel this is your home? Do you feel at peace here on this planet? Or do you feel oddly ill at ease on Earth for some undefined or unspecified reason? If you do, then you just might want to consider the idea that we, as a hybridized species perhaps, came from elsewhere. Just possibly, that "elsewhere" might have been Mars. Alternatively, it might have been some place even farther away....

CONCLUSION

We have covered a lot in this book about Mars and information related to that planet. Everything from the statistics about Mars, Mars anomalies, the moons of Mars, the geology, to ancient aliens, and even conspiracy theories about Mars have been included here. As interesting as all this might be, what conclusions, if any, can we draw from all of this information? Moreover, can we draw any conclusions at all?

Well, we can draw quite a number, I think. We know, for instance, that Mars is not the world that it once was. Now, it is cold and dry compared to having been once warmer, wetter, with a thicker atmosphere, and protective magnetic field around it. The Mars of today is very different from the Mars that once was. That much seems certain.

Additionally, we have more information these days about the two moons of Mars and this is recent data. Although, the origins of the little moons seems shrouded in mystery. Are they asteroids? Possibly, but how did they get into the orbits around Mars, if they are? This has defied the ability of current astronomers and cosmologists to solve.

Furthermore, the moon, Phobos, is decidedly strange! It appears to be hollow or at least we cannot otherwise account for its too-low density. Besides which, Phobos orbits Mars more swiftly than any other moon around any other planet in our solar system. This includes Earth's Moon. Phobos also has an extremely close orbit to Mars and at times, the moon's orbit actually appears to slow down some and then speed up again. Although different researchers claim this might be an illusion of sorts, nobody seems to know for sure.

We also know Phobos has those odd grooves and chains of craters, which some researchers theorize might actually be the result of someone or "something" having set off some type of explosions or detonations on the surface there to move the moon to its present orbit, to steer it into position around Mars. Actually, it would make an ideal location for observation, even as our Moon makes the same thing with regard to Earth.

If this is so, if we can determine whether if this is true or not, then we have our "smoking gun" regarding extraterrestrial life being, or having been at some point in the past, in our solar system. Additionally, this one explanation fits all the facts, whereas none other seems to be able to do this. If we follow the Principle of Occam's Razor, as most scientists and researchers do, then we have to take the simplest explanation that explains all the facts and not choose ones that are more convoluted.

Mars itself is also a strange little planet. As I've mentioned, the southern half of the planet has a generally higher altitude than the northern half. The planet has the largest volcano (Olympus Mons) by far of any planet in the solar system, and the largest canyon (Valles Marineris), as well.

There are signs Mars was devastated and so lost its warmer and wetter environment. Yet, there is still some water there. Furthermore, the orbit of Mars is highly elliptical. The orbit is also in a slightly different plane than other planets. Yet, scientists cannot account for why this is. They theorize, but have no hard evidence to back up their theories.

Again, we have even more of these types of oddities, as well. Not just Phobos is strange, but we have anomalies all over Mars itself that are equally strange. There are what look like train tracks almost, even with "something" sitting on or right next to them.

We have other straight lines that shouldn't be there, for which nobody can account.

In addition, we have what appear to be ruins, but also other items that still look intact, such as the domes (with and without windows in them), three towers widely and evenly spaced that seem to reach about the height of almost a mile, and even more such "towers" some distance from those. They have a metallic or smooth look to their top because they are highly reflective, unlike other natural formations in the area.

Additionally, there are what appear to be ruins on Mars, including those of pyramids, fortresses, cities and much more. Yes, many of them might be just the human eye trying to see patterns where there is none, but others do seem to be there, and do look like actual ruins. We even have what seems to be the ruins of an underground city (the grid pattern mentioned earlier in the book) that might still be radioactive and so giving off heat. Some way or other, it is radiating heat and that much is a certainty. The only questions are how and why. The answers to this are limited to either volcanic (and we see no sign of this there), or again, radioactive sources.

There are other weird things about Mars, as well. Some photos, such as the "lizard" on the Rover are hard to explain. There are also photos that look like they might be forests, or even herds of some kind of animal migrating across a plain. We've seen photos of monoliths, what resemble statues, and even bones, even one that could be an elongated skull.

Other anomalies include radioactive isotopes spread over the planet's surface that had to have come from some sort of nuclear explosions, whether caused by intelligent beings or by a very large "natural" georeactor. This has caused one scientist, Dr. Brandenburg, to become convinced there was a nuclear war on Mars and this destroyed the planet's atmosphere and biosphere. He further is convinced that there might have been two native races on Mars, the Cydonians and the Utopians.

If those who back the Anunnaki theory of ancient aliens on Earth and Mars are correct, then one of the races on Mars, as Dr. Brandenburg claims, might have been them, the Anunnaki, and the other one...us, as slave laborers.

In any case, whatever the situation was so long ago, we have no doubt Mars is not the planet it once was, and that is almost a certainty. The red planet does seem to have undergone massive changes, and the question is, just how long ago did these occur? Was it billions, millions of years ago, or just a few tens of thousands? Again, we just don't know the answer to that yet. Researchers can only make guesses and those seem all over the place.

There are other things about Mars for which we simply cannot account. There are those weird fountains of lights, those glows that appear to erupt from the ground and glow skyward, and have been photographed by NASA's Rover. There is the image of "something" flying through the Martian skies, more than once, and it isn't orbiting in outer space, but well within the atmosphere. It most definitely <u>does not look</u> to be a meteor, asteroid, or comet, either. In other words, the UFO doesn't appear to be a "natural" object. So just what is it? The thing actually seems to resemble some type of aircraft when one zooms in on the photographs.

We also have the mysterious shadows on Mars, such as the one that so closely resembles the Black Knight Satellite of Earth, supposedly. Then there are the Russian Fobos 2 photos sent to Earth just before "something" impacted the satellite, sending it into an uncontrolled spin and then destructing. Those photos reveal a long cylinder shaped object near the moon,

Phobos, and what's more, the thing even cast a shadow down onto Mars and this shadow moved across the surface of the planet. Therefore, we know it was, indeed, a shadow of something from above! Then there is the matter of photographs from around Neptune and Saturn also sometimes showing in the distance cylinder-like "somethings" in orbit there, as well.

Moreover, there are the conspiracy theories about a secret space fleet, Solar Warden, perhaps with Orion-style ships of huge dimensions. We have testimony of several people who say they were involved, one way, or the other, with such a space fleet, and that they were stationed on Mars for years.

Evidence seems to exist something like a space fleet just might exist, such as those pixelated photos of "something" by the sun, not just one object, but a number of them in different locations there. Then there is President Reagan's strange diary notation saying we can loft 300 people into space at once, when NASA simply wasn't supposedly capable of such a feat then or even now.

We have the reports by a number of astronauts, along with photos and even videos of strange "somethings" near Earth orbit, on the Moon, and farther afield. There are reports by many astronauts, former NASA officials, and retired military officers, as well as even the former governor of Arizona that "something" extraterrestrial seems to be going on. We have test pilots who claim part of their task was to film the UFOs they encountered.

We also have numerous conspiracy theories, some with a partial ring of truth to them, such as people claiming to have been teleported to Mars, as in Project Pegasus, or having served in that space fleet on and near the red planet. Several people, independent of each other, have claimed this teleportation.

There is also the matter of the remote viewers, which a released CIA document claims to have been well worth the time and money spent on researching them, and that remote viewing should be a regular part of our information (espionage) program. The document stating this is included here in this book. Moreover, one famous remote viewer, Ingo Swann, insists he saw Mars of old, over a million years ago, with intelligent lifeforms on the planet, and then in a later time, the planet having "something" in the way of a huge catastrophe. He is not the only remote viewer to claim that such talents seem to be "outside" of space and time, that they are not restricted to just viewing things in the "here and now."

We also aren't even sure what caused the catastrophe of Mars. Was it a nuclear war, one promulgated by yet another alien race intent on wiping out all intelligent life that might be thought of as competition for them? On the other hand, was it the destruction of a fifth planet, "Phaeton," that sent chunks of planetary shrapnel in the form of an asteroid or asteroids that destroyed Mars? Alternatively, was it "something" entirely different? Was Mars pulled from its original orbit somehow, and so suffered a slow death, punctuated by an asteroid impact or nuclear war at the end?

Have you noticed there seem to be a deluge of "somethings" here and we aren't sure just what they are, what they are about, or what they all mean. Mostly, what we have are questions about them. Yet with so much available information, so many thousands of photographs, videos, eyewitness testimonies, deathbed confessions and such, it's hard not to arrive at the one conclusion that makes sense of it all:

That conclusion is there are extraterrestrials. Not only do they seem to be here on Earth and in our skies, but throughout our solar system, as well. There seems no way around this conclusion, at least, not for me. The evidence is just too overwhelming on this point.

For me, extraterrestrials are almost a certainty. Again, I base this on applying the Principle of Occam's Razor, since that answer is the least complicated of any others (so far), and answers all the questions and not just some of them. However, you must decide this for yourselves, come up with your own conclusions about it all. I have merely provided information here and my own conclusions and opinions, but they are just that, only my opinions.

Furthermore, it does appear that Mars might be immediately involved in all this, not only now, in the present, but in the distant past, as well. Even we humans might be involved in the distant past with Mars. Dr. Ellis Silver claimed we humans might even be hybridized (even as the ancient Sumerians claimed), and probably came from a different planet. In fact, his description of human problems on Earth, bad backs, sun burning, etc. all make it sound as if we came from a smaller planet with less gravity, and a weaker or more distant sun...meaning Mars?

Were we the true Martians? Are we still? Alternatively, were we one of the two races on Mars? Did we flee the catastrophe of Mars as a few ragtag refugees, only to settle on a primitive planet we were not truly suited for, then through the ages forgot our history, and acquired a form of racial amnesia?

It has happened before. The British, within just two to three generations of them leaving, forgot the Romans had ever occupied their territory. They thought Hadrian's Wall, ordered built by the Roman Emperor, Hadrian, had been the work of a race of giants. So racial amnesia is a real thing.

Again, there are many unanswered questions and many scenarios for the mystery that is Mars. However, despite all the variations, some main themes do seem to be well supported.

Mars is a planet that suffered a major catastrophe. How long ago this happened is a matter of debate. There are anomalies on Mars for which we, at this stage, simply can't account. There is a high failure rate for missions to Mars, far higher than any other planet in the solar system, and this just shouldn't be.

There are definitely weird photos, such as those of Fobos 2, for which we still cannot find an answer (other than the obvious one...extraterrestrials or perhaps, even humans?). The moon, Phobos, is perhaps the oddest moon (besides our own, actually) of any moon in the solar system.

There is the massive canyon, the Valles Marineris, and we have no explanation for how this came to be. All we know is that it is gigantic in proportions and deep, and just as Olympus Mons is gargantuan and high, as well.

Additionally, there are many more such things to consider, but these should suffice for us here, to show just how strange, just how bizarrely marvelous, yes, and even just how spooky Mars might be.

Is there intelligent life besides our own? I would have to say yes, given all the data I've seen as a MUFON investigator. Is there intelligent life on or near Mars? Again, I would have to give a qualified yes to this. Have we humans in the past interacted with such extraterrestrial life? It would seem, judging by worldwide legends, the Sumerian cuneiform writings, the Vedic Texts, that we might very well have and on numerous occasions.

Has this interaction been to our benefit? I would have to say no, it has not been, given the radioactive sites situated around India, including the Lonar Crater, the ruins of Mohenjo-Daro, as well as Harappa, and even other places. Whatever happened long ago, it didn't seem to be a good thing for us, but instead, "something" bad, perhaps a human rebellion and resulting war on Earth, or even an interplanetary or interstellar war besides this.

Are we in danger from extraterrestrials now, here and perhaps on Mars? Again, I'd have to say we have reason definitely to be worried about this idea. UFO interactions here on Earth have often not been promising, have caused damage to property, resulted in illnesses, and even death for those involved in such interactions with extraterrestrials. That's not even counting the million plus who claim to have been abducted against their wills by the aliens. Therefore, why should we believe extraterrestrial behavior might be any different or better on Mars?

This leads us to the question if extraterrestrials still inhabit the red planet. This is harder to say, but if UFOs in the skies of Mars is anything to go by, then perhaps, they are still there, whoever "they" might be. In which case, we should be very careful about how we proceed with our explorations of that world and perhaps even more importantly, the moon Phobos.

Why do I say this? Well, the whole history of UFOs, sightings, interactions, etc., on our world have not been what I would call a good or positive thing overall. They seem to avoid interacting with us in any sort of an open way, and yet they seem to do whatever they want, for good or ill (mostly ill, it seems to me) with an arrogant impunity, a callous disregard for our rights as sentient human beings.

If aliens inhabit Mar, or have a base on Phobos in its interior, which would offer them more protection from radiation and discovery by us, then we had better tread carefully, very carefully. If they see us as a threat, we might well be powerless to protect ourselves, even as our governments don't seem to be able to protect our airspace, or even their own citizens from these creatures.

Mind you, I am not saying we shouldn't continue our explorations of Mars. We should. However, I do think great care should be exercised in this regard. Perhaps, that is exactly what our government is doing by hiding things, not telling the whole truth about it all, in an effort to safeguard us from the effects of such an incredible revelation. Worse, if the extraterrestrials decide we know too much, they might simply appear *en masse* and no longer worry about trying to hide themselves in any way from us. This means they might increase their activities, as well, which again, might not be good for humans at all!

Or course, there is even a worse scenario in this regard. That is, the extraterrestrials just don't care about us at all, literally don't give a damn what we think, do, or say, which could well be within the realm of possibility. If they are advanced as their craft seem to imply, they might simply see us as perhaps their ancestors, the Anunnaki as we've called them did…in other words, just a slave-labor pool, ready for the taking at any time.

I don't have all the answers to these questions, but I am convinced the extraterrestrials are real, have been on Mars, at least in the past, and might well even be there now. We have much to learn from Mars in this regard. However, we should make certain they aren't all the wrong lessons…

Finally, I leave it to each reader to take all this information in, consider it at some length, I hope, and then reach his or her own conclusions. These conclusions might be diametrically opposed to my own ideas on these issues, but that's fine. That's what this is all about. The more people willing to learn about these things, to sift through the available information, and the more who are willing to search for answers and to ponder the issues, the better chance we all have of reaching some real conclusions...one way or the other.

In the meantime, when you look up at the night sky and see that little glowing red star, the Planet Mars, just keep one thing in mind; its name, "Mars," is called so for the god of war, and it just might be more appropriate than any of us might imagine...

END

ABOUT THE AUTHOR

Rob Shelsky is an avid and eclectic writer, and averages about 4,000 words a day. Rob, with a degree in science, has written a large number of factual articles for the former *AlienSkin Magazine*, as well as for other magazines, such as *Doorways, Midnight Street* (U.K.), *Internet Review of Science Fiction (IROSF),* and many others. While at AlienSkin Magazine, a resident columnist there for about seven years, Rob did a number of investigative articles, including some concerning the paranormal, as well as columns about UFOs, including interviews of those who have had encounters with them.

Rob has been interviewed on a large number of shows, including George Noory's Coast-To-Coast AM Radio show, House of Mystery, The Kevin Cook Show, and many others. He has often and over a long period, explored the alien and UFO question and has made investigative trips to research such UFO hotspot areas as Pine Bush, New York, Gulf Breeze, Florida, and other such regions, including Brown Mountain, North Carolina, known, for the infamous "Brown Mountain Lights, as well as investigating numerous places known for paranormal activity. He has traveled abroad to do this, as well, as with traveling to sites in the United Kingdom, as well as other countries where UFOs have been reported. Rob is a member of MUFON, and a Field Investigator for this group. The author was even invited to speak at the Library of Congress, Washington D.C. His nonfiction books on paranormal topics are many.

With over 20 years of such research and investigative efforts behind him, Author Rob Shelsky is well qualified in the subject of UFOs, as well as that of the paranormal. Where Rob Shelsky tends to be the skeptic, and insists upon being able to "kick the tires" of a UFO, to ascertain their reality, he is, as well, a theorist, constantly coming up with possible explanations for various such phenomena. Rob asks the hard questions others seem to avoid. Often, he comes up with convincing answers.

For links to Robs other books on the subject of UFOs, please go to:

Or: **http://robshelsky.blogspot.com/**

REFERENCE LIST

Martian meteorite with fossil remains:
https://www2.jpl.nasa.gov/snc/nasa1.html
Viking II Mars Mission:
**http://news.nationalgeographic.com/news/201
2/04/120413-nasa-viking-program-mars-life-
space-science/**
"City of Cydonia:
**https://www.google.com/search?q=INFRARED
+PHOTOS+OF+AN+UNDERGROUND+CITY+on+
mars&tbm=isch&imgil=ar1zu7pcylFoCM%253A
%253BwwjsN7IoKku2XM%253Bhttp%25253A
%25252F%25252Fwww.enterprisemission.com
%25252Fir_analysis.html&source=iu&pf=m&fir
=ar1zu7pcylFoCM%253A%252CwwjsN7IoKku2
XM%252C_&usg=___K-
cYm2JNuQKfktkAMKQ3LiirXzA%3D&biw=1195&
bih=578&ved=0ahUKEwjW5uLU0InWAhUI7iYKH
RvrDwMQyjcIMQ&ei=zUesWZbMA4jcmwGb1r8Y
#imgrc=kFYafIviatIqEM**:
Statues on Mars:
**http://www.express.co.uk/news/weird/745731
/Mars-STATUES-relics-ancient-Martian-
civilisation**
Martian anomalies:
**http://www.theblackvault.com/casefiles/categ
ory/space-anomalies/mars-anomalies/**
Asteroid impact on Mars.
**https://www.scientificamerican.com/article/gia
nt-asteroid-collision-may-have-radically-
transformed-mars/**
Dr. Brandenburg, nuclear war on Mars:
**http://www.dailymail.co.uk/sciencetech/article
-2843871/Ancient-Martian-civilisation-wiped-**

nuclear-bomb-wielding-aliens-attack-Earth-claims-physicist.html#ixzz4jAlVL7dg

Vedic Texts:
https://en.wikipedia.org/wiki/Brahmastra

Mohenjo-Daro and Harappa:
http://www.nationalgeographic.com/archaeology-and-history/archaeology/mohenjo-daro/

Wrong commands sent to Orbiter by NASA:
http://www.cnn.com/TECH/space/9909/30/mars.metric.02/

Ancient Martian City:
https://www.thesun.co.uk/news/1968291/nasa-curiosity-rover-photo-shows-ruins-of-walled-city-once-inhabited-by-aliens-on-mars/

Deadly UFOs and the Disappeared:
https://www.amazon.com/Deadly-UFOs-Disappeared-Rob-Shelsky-ebook/dp/B00TZ98K9U

Electric Universe Theory:
http://www.electricuniverse.info/Introduction

Alien lizard?
http://www.express.co.uk/news/weird/782473/NASA-Curiosity-rover-Mars-lizard

Martian UFO:
http://www.express.co.uk/news/science/618478/First-aliens-UFO-found-flying-surface-Mars-NASA-photos-space-Curiosity-Rover

Stone Circle On Mars:
http://www.foxnews.com/tech/2017/06/21/strange-stone-circle-spotted-on-mars.html

Black Knight shadow on Mars:
http://www.seattlepi.com/local/science/article/Shadow-on-Mars-resembles-infamous-Black-Knight-11089307.php#photo-12768514

Secret space shuttle:
https://www.theatlantic.com/technology/archive/2017/05/why-so-secretive/525969/

Renaissance painting with UFO:
http://proofofalien.com/alien-evidences-of-the-madonna-with-saint-giovannino/
Martian train tracks:
http://www.marsanomalyresearch.com/evidence-reports/2011/208/tracks-n-water.htm
Martian train tracks:
http://alfredsnider.blogspot.com/2011/11/martian-railroad.html
Spaceship over the sun:
http://www.dailymail.co.uk/sciencetech/article-2142570/YouTube-user-accuses-NASA-coverup-finds-UFO-hovering-near-Sun.html
Dr. Brandenburg's Nuclear theory of Mars:
http://www.dailymail.co.uk/sciencetech/article-3339949/Mystery-DOME-Mars-Alien-hunters-say-structure-built-ancient-civilisation-red-planet.html#ixzz4jAljlCQx
Are humans aliens:
http://www.dailymail.co.uk/sciencetech/article-2507377/Humans-NOT-come-Earth--sunburn-bad-backs-pain-labour-prove-expert-claims.html
Planet "5:"
https://www.google.com/search?q=What+was+the+name+of+the+fifth+planet+that+caused+the+asteroid+belt%3F&ie=utf-8&oe=utf-8
Project Orion:
https://www.nasa.gov/audience/forstudents/5-8/features/nasa-knows/what-is-orion-58.html
Solar Warden:
https://www.theepochtimes.com/the-solar-warden-covert-space-project-fact-or-science-fiction_1253536.html
Solar Warden:
https://truedisclosure.org/news/solar-warden-inception-to-present-day.html
Anunnaki: **https://www.annunaki.org/**

http://www.theancientaliens.com/433000-years-of-annunaki-rule

Rh Negative Presidents and Royal Blood:

http://www.sentinelprogress.com/opinion/columns/6748/not-to-be-negative-but

Rh Negative Trump:

http://www.rhesusnegative.net/staynegative/donald-trump-rh-negative/

Rh Negative Presidents:

https://www.youtube.com/watch?v=o-n5OAj8b5Y4

Rh Negative Theories:

http://www.rhnegativeregistry.com/Rh_Negative_Factor_Blood_Origin_Theories_Migration.html

Rh Negative people have alien blood:

https://truththeory.com/2016/10/08/blood-type-dna-might-just-alien/

Rh Negative not from our planet:

https://www.pinterest.com/pin/546342998529923988/

Cydonia:

https://en.wikipedia.org/wiki/Cydonia_(region_of_Mars)

Mars Utopians:

http://www.ibtimes.co.uk/interplanetary-genocide-martian-civilisations-wiped-out-by-nuclear-attacks-1476348

Deadly UFOs And The Disappeared:

https://www.amazon.com/Deadly-UFOs-Disappeared-Rob-Shelsky/dp/1508633460/ref=tmm_pap_swatch_0?_encoding=UTF8&qid=&sr=

Men walking on Mars:

http://www.dailymail.co.uk/sciencetech/article-2852829/Was-secret-manned-mission-Mars-

1979-Former-Nasa-employee-claims-saw-suited-men-running-red-planet.html

War on Mars: **http://www.ibtimes.co.uk/interplanetary-genocide-martian-civilisations-wiped-out-by-nuclear-attacks-1476348**

Martian war: **https://motherboard.vice.com/en_us/article/9aknn8/were-ancient-martians-murdered-by-nuclear-bomb-dropping-aliens-an-investigation**

Planet Phaeton: **http://www.guide-to-the-universe.com/planet-phaeton.html**

Phaeton: **http://www.ldolphin.org/unruh/planet/order.html**

The fifth planet: **http://www.abovetopsecret.com/forum/thread908541/pg1**

Refueling at sun: **http://www.section51-ufo.com/2016/09/strange-video-from-nasa-shows-ufo-mothership-refueling-at-the-sun-sept-2016.html**

SOHO images of alien ships at sun: **https://www.nasa.gov/content/goddard/soho-sees-something-new-near-the-sun**

Alien ships near sun: **http://www.dailymail.co.uk/sciencetech/article-4001140/Are-aliens-harvesting-energy-sun-UFO-hunters-claim-evidence-star-lifting-Nasa-images.html**

Anunnaki on Mars: **https://www.ancient-code.com/the-ancient-anunnaki-and-the-mars-connection/**

Statues on Mars: **http://www.disclose.tv/news/has_nasa_discovered_an_annunaki_statue_on_mars/138643**

Mars and Sitchin:
http://www.sitchin.com/nasa_looking.htm
Radioactive Mohenjo-Daro: **http://www.ancient-origins.net/ancient-places-asia/mohenjo-daro-massacre-00819**
Mohenjo-Daro:
http://www.nationalgeographic.com/archaeology-and-history/archaeology/mohenjo-daro/
Mohenjo-Daro:
http://earthmysterynews.com/2016/10/19/evidences-of-nuclear-explosion-in-mohenjo-daro/
Harappa: **https://learnodo-newtonic.com/indus-valley-civilization-facts**
Rama Empire: **http://eden-saga.com/en/india-archeology-indus-harappa-mohenjodaro-mahabalipuram-adam-s-bridge-ceylon-the-empire-of-rama.html**
10,000 year old civilization:
http://www.abovetopsecret.com/forum/thread98945/pg1
Ancient civilization:
https://www.thebetterindia.com/60143/mohenjodaro-harappa-indus-valley-civilization/
Alpha Centauri planets:
https://www.newscientist.com/article/dn27259-twin-earths-may-lurk-in-our-nearest-star-system/
Origin of Mars:
http://science.howstuffworks.com/mars2.htm
Jupiter's orbit changes:
https://www.space.com/28901-wandering-jupiter-oddball-solar-system.html
Rogue planets:
http://www.express.co.uk/news/world/753174/planets-astronomers-ninth-rogue-solar-system-aliens-galaxy-space

Rogue planets between stars:
http://www.pbs.org/newshour/rundown/billio ns-rogue-planets-wander-universe-without- home/
Faster than light travel:
http://www.escapistmagazine.com/articles/vie w/scienceandtech/columns/forscience/11746- 5-Faster-Than-Light-Travel-Methods-and-Their- Plausibility
FTL: **https://en.wikipedia.org/wiki/Faster-than- light**
Superluminal drives:
https://www.popsci.com/superluminal
Formation of solar system:
https://www.windows2universe.org/our_solar_ system/formation.html
Solar system stability:
https://en.wikipedia.org/wiki/Stability_of_the_ Solar_System
Atomic powered rockets:
https://gizmodo.com/5992441/how-nasas- nuclear-rockets-will-take-us-way-beyond-mars
Advanced atomic rockets:
https://www.nasa.gov/topics/technology/featu res/ntrees.html
Martian whistleblower:
http://exopolitics.org/whistleblowers-claims- he-served-17-years-at-secret-mars-military- base/
Secret base on Mars:
http://www.mirror.co.uk/news/weird- news/secret-alien-base-mars-marine-3745652
Captain Kaye:
http://www.disclose.tv/news/US_soldier_claim s_he_has_spent_17_years_battling_ALIENS_on _Mars/111519

Captain Kaye:
https://www.gaia.com/article/randy-cramer-mars-defense-force
Captain Kaye, hoax or real: **http://freedom-articles.toolsforfreedom.com/mars-whistleblowers-captain-kaye/**
Secret base on Moon:
http://uncyclopedia.wikia.com/wiki/Secret_Moon_Base
Secret bases on Moon:
http://www.popularmechanics.com/space/moon-mars/a19405/ussr-1960s-lunar-base/
Secret bases on Moon:
http://www.ufosightingsdaily.com/2012/03/moon-structures-alien-bases-caught-on.html
Congressman ask Nasa about ancient civilizations on Mars: **https://www.cnet.com/news/mars-nasa-congress-hearing-aliens-rohrabacher-rover-civilizations/**
Alien ships near sun:
https://www.inquisitr.com/2564622/massive-alien-cruise-ship-ufo-passes-between-earth-and-sun-in-nasa-soho-image/
DNA of elongated skulls:
http://www.express.co.uk/news/weird/694326/Are-these-alien-skulls-New-DNA-tests-on-Elongated-Paracas-Skulls-could-change-history
Paracas skulls: **http://www.ancient-origins.net/news-evolution-human-origins/initial-dna-analysis-paracas-elongated-skull-released-incredible**
Ancient rulers with elongated skulls:
http://www.messagetoeagle.com/mysterious-ancient-rulers-with-elongated-skulls-who-were-they-really/

Printed in Great Britain
by Amazon

87312634R00155